Mícheál Mac Gabhann ???

The Divorced Catholic

EDMUND FLOOD is an editor of *Living Parish Pamphlets* and of *The Sower*, and is a founder member of the Catholic Theological Association of Great Britain. He has written extensively on Scripture and Theology, and has given talks on St Paul in Australia, Canada, New Zealand and the United Kingdom.

GW00712328

EDMUND FLOOD

The Divorced Catholic

Collins
FOUNT PAPERBACKS

Contents

Our Need To Explore

Most of us have experienced the pain that comes from the ending of a marriage. Whether in our own family or in those of friends, we've known the impact it can have on people's lives.

We also know that Western countries have a serious divorce problem. We know that about one in every two or three marriages end in divorce – even Catholic ones – and we appreciate the need both of couples and of children to experience faithful love. Psychology has taught us to value stable marriage more than ever, just when it is so widely under threat.

For Christians especially, all this raises urgent questions. We have been called to live as Jesus did and be "a light to the world" (Philippians 2:16). What does that oblige us to with regard to marriage and divorce?

Some Christians have a simple answer about divorce. "Christ forbade divorce, so it is always wrong. Our job as Christians is therefore always to condemn it. And Christians who divorce and remarry are no longer Jesus' followers and cannot be admitted to the Eucharist."

Other Christians wonder whether that does justice to reality. They have Christian friends who have re-married after a divorce and who lead admirable Christian lives. Jesus said strong things about marriage and divorce; but the reason it became "necessary" to have him executed was that he put compassion to the afflicted and to sinners before the law. Is it so sure that these people should be barred from the Christian table?

Other questions arise. We realize that today especially the Church has a great responsibility to stand for true marriage by the way its members live. But can marriages become "dead"? And, if the answer is "Sometimes, yes", does forcing Christians by law to remain in "dead" marriages help or hinder Christ's purpose? Is this the witness to true marriage that Jesus intended and that the world can understand?

Any body that stands for truth needs to ask questions. What we stand for is the deepest truth about human reality in the light of God's revelation. Always we need to deepen our understanding of that reality and that revelation, and to face the challenges that raises for us. How else can we fulfil our role as Christians in a world that needs evidence that Christianity offers it the truth about itself?

Bishops and theologians are leading us in this questioning direction. That became clearest in 1980. In the Synod of that year, bishops came to Rome from all over the world to re-examine with the Pope the Church's ministry and theology with regard to marriage. There was no dearth of searching questions. "The fact that divorces increased dramatically is in itself a reason for restudying the requirements for a valid marriage, taking into account the findings of modern psychology, especially regarding the condition for freedom, maturity and commitment." "We have an obligation to re-examine certain aspects of doctrine upon which the indissolubility of marriage is based." These questions came from a Canadian archbishop (Archbishop Henri Legare).

Archbishop Worlock of Liverpool spoke in the name of

the bishops of England and Wales: "Many pastors nowadays are faced with Catholics whose first marriages have perished and who have now a second and more stable (if legally only civil) union in which they seek to bring up a new family. Often such persons, especially in their desire to help their children, long for the restoration of full eucharistic communion with the Church and its Lord. Is this spirit of repentance and desire for sacramental strength to be forever frustrated? Can they be told only that they must reject their new responsibilities as a necessary condition for forgiveness and restoration to sacramental life?"

The bishops who asked such questions were not seeking to dilute Jesus' teaching. They asked them because they had reason to doubt whether we have sufficiently understood that teaching. And the bluntness of their questions arose from a deep fear. If, in some important respects, we have misunderstood Jesus' teaching, are we forcing the lives of Christians into a straightjacket of *our own* devising? Are we causing so much suffering unnecessarily? Are we bringing into disrepute, by doing so, what Jesus wants to say not just to ourselves but to the whole world?

Facing up to the truth about yourself is arduous and sometimes painful. But it leads, in the end, to a sense of freedom and rebirth. In the matter of divorce, and much else, we have embarked on that process.

We are asking what the Word of God is saying to us today. The New Testament called that "prophecy". A prophet did not so much foretell the future as enable the Church community to apply Christ's message to its present situation and opportunities. No wonder Paul considered that gift the most valuable of all!

All Christians have a prophetic gift and a prophetic task, and, in marriage matters, families particularly have it. "This prophetic mission of the family, and so of husbands and wives, is based upon their experience as married persons and on an understanding of the sacrament of marriage with which they can speak with their own authority. This experience and this understanding contribute, I would suggest, an authentic source of theology from which we, the pastors, and indeed the whole Church can draw" (Archbishop Derek Worlock).

Firm answers may not come quickly. The new insights we have about Scripture and about human relationships take time to absorb and apply to our practices.

But patience is required in every important exploration. What matters in this one is that we try to be open to the Spirit, listen respectfully to one another, and travel humbly together.

This book seeks to set out these new insights and so be a guide for our exploration.

PART 1

The Data

1.

Marriage and Divorce Today

Strength and Vulnerability

A cartoon in *The New Yorker* put the question vividly and succinctly. You saw a large young man sitting on one side of a bar table and a pretty young girl facing him on the other. "Allison, will you be my *first* wife?" was the caption.

It's not only *The New Yorker*, of course, that can be cynical about marriage. The divorce statistics are astronomical and widely known. We know that behind many of them is the human misery of a marriage falling apart, and a sense of great loss and even powerlessness. We also know that it is on their marriage that most people depend for their personal happiness and fulfilment.

Why is marriage today much more vulnerable? Most of this chapter will explore the reasons. But it's first necessary to get our enquiry into focus. It's not one of total gloom and despondency. We're like rich young people who still have a lot to learn about handling their wealth. This book is much more about wealth than poverty.

I think we see this even in that vulnerability. It's true that divorce is often caused by weakness. But isn't a bigger cause our strength – or our potential strength? We want more from marriage than most of our grandparents ever dreamed was possible. The evidence about second marriages shows that even people whose first marriages have failed still expect to get it. Now that we are learning so much more about the reality of contemporary Western marriage – what can make it lasting and happy and how it can fail – we should usually be able to realize our strength.

So, in order to understand divorce, we must first consider marriage. What are its contemporary strengths? And what makes it today especially vulnerable?

Christian Marriage

To start in this way is particularly necessary when we're talking about *Christian* marriage. Christianity is about God becoming accessible to all men and women, first in the life of Jesus and now in us, his body. Our job as Christians is to manifest to the world, in the way we live, *God's* kind of life: his love, his compassion, his faithfulness. We are called to show the world that there is hope and meaning.

That's the way God works! He doesn't show the world who he is through extraordinary appearances or even, primarily, through laws. He takes human form. First, a man of Nazareth. Then us. Then a meal with its joy and companionship. Then the other sacraments. Sacraments are simply God showing himself in some key part of human reality. In the New Testament Jesus is called "the image – the human projection – of God" (2 Corinthians 4:4; Colossians 1:15). That was only another way of saying that Jesus is *the* sacrament.

One of our greatest discoveries in the last few decades is this human realism and warmth with which

14

God always seeks to approach us. Not me as a statistic, but me as the individual I am, with my own strengths and weaknesses, that is the person with whom God wants to be intimate. This strategy is deeply embedded in the New Testament, and, though often hiddenly, in the history of the Church. We shall see how much it is at the forefront of the recent developments in Catholic understanding of divorce.

A Christian couple's married life is one of the human forms that God's presence takes. Given that most people marry, it is one of the chief ways God seeks to be manifest and accessible to the world that wants evidence that there is a God who brings peace and joy and love and faithfulness. John and Jane, as married Christians, try to let the Spirit of the risen Christ bear fruit in their married lives. In so far as that happens, they will show the warm human presence of God in them.

So, when we call their marriage a "sacrament", we're not talking directly about the wedding ceremony, but of the reality of two people's lives together. The only important questions for their own experience of marriage and for everyone concerned are: Do their lives together show God's loving, creative presence? and, How can that be made more possible?

John and Jane live a 1980, Western-world kind of married life. They are likely, for instance, to live into their seventies, both have jobs at some stages of their married life, and both have certain expectations of fulfilment and equality in marriage. It is in this kind of context that their love, their faithfulness and all their other qualities can be the place where sacrament happens: where God becomes manifested and enjoyed, as he was in Jesus. And it's in this context, too, where it is possible that they do not – and perhaps even cannot – withstand the stresses and strains that this kind of married life is prone to.

So our reflection on Christian marriage and divorce doesn't take us into a bizarre kind of world of theological notions. The reflection must consist in our focusing accurately on this one. What, then, are the contemporary strengths of marriage in our kind of culture? And what makes it today especially vulnerable?

The Strengths and the Attendant Risks

Winston Churchill, as a child, greatly admired his father. But only twice in his life was he given the opportunity of a serious talk with him. In the upper and middle classes, children called their father "Sir". The level of intimacy within families naturally differed widely; and, even in 1845, not every wife's advice would have been the same as Mrs Ellis': "Suffer and be still"! But it's only in the last four decades that intimate affection between the couple has generally been seen as the heart of a good marriage. And it's only in the last decade or two that some of the practical implications of that have begun to be clear.

Today, therefore, a married person has an outstanding opportunity. He or she can find happiness and grow as a person through a deep and close relationship and an equal partnership in seeking happiness and fulfilment. On the other hand, a voyage through largely unchartered waters is hazardous – especially a long and varied one. And many of the supports that would earlier have helped that journey have gone.

So there are two sides to the situation of a modern

couple. We'll understand both sides more clearly if we start by comparing their situation with that of the recent past.

1 *The focus changes from child-bearing*

A century ago, the average length of life for most classes was about thirty-eight years for a woman and thirty-six years for a man. Because of the high rate of infant and child mortality, a large number of pregnancies were necessary if enough children were to reach adult age. The woman's married life was therefore mainly engaged in bearing and raising children.

Today's situation is, of course, entirely different. Both partners are likely to live to over seventy. A low infant mortality rate and the current preference for a family of two or so children will mean that child-bearing will occupy a small number of years. The couple has far more time for each other, even before the children have left home. The modern expectations of intimacy and equal sharing will help to motivate them to want to develop a full relationship.

The couple's opportunities for a happy partnership are therefore much richer. But of course the earlier kind of marriage was much safer from obvious failure. Since it usually had no high expectations of intimacy, couples were much less apt to have a sense of frustration or even imprisonment than is common today. And, with the low life expectancy, a couple would probably not have to tackle together the changes that often come to us in our forties.

2 *Cohesion no longer from the social setting*

There is another important respect in which the modern kind of marriage has both greater opportunities and higher risks. Until fairly recently the social setting tended to keep in existence even very unsuccessful marriages. Particularly in the country, the family home was within the work-place itself or was closely connected with it. The lives of the whole family were in one way or another centred on the same work, and for purely economic reasons it could be almost unthinkable to part. Another factor was the closeknit local community. It was likely to run on the assumption that almost all couples would somehow stay together, however cold their relationship might happen to be.

A modern couple, by contrast, is likely to be on their own, and their jobs are likely to be different from each other's. So there aren't those strong pressures from their work-place and their neighbourhood to keep them together.

On the positive side, this means that their fidelity will come from themselves, not from economic or social forces. It also means that each can contribute to their life together the experience of a different kind of job. The developments in their own character as they tackle the challenges their jobs can bring can widen their shared interests and enrich their relationship.

On the negative side is the danger that they may get so absorbed in their jobs that they find themselves living in totally different worlds. Especially at any crisis points in the development of their marriage, the consequences can be grave.

Marriage is a Long Journey – Not Always In Step

The crisis points just mentioned are at the centre of our contemporary divorce problems, especially for Christians. A sincere Christian wants to show love and be faithful to his or her spouse. But two questions arise about that. The first is whether that sincere desire is invariably enough to save a real marriage, in the face of the more devastating of those crisis points. The second question arises if our answer to that has to be "Sometimes, no". If the marriage relationship really becomes an empty husk, can something so different from what the Church now understands by marriage really remain one?

Few people have done more to elucidate these crisis points than Dr Jack Dominian, a Catholic psychiatrist. Himself a saintly man, he is widely regarded by many as a prophet in these matters.

First, he reminds us of some important aspects of married life which are already fairly obvious but provide the context for what follows[1].

If married life essentially consists in two people finding growth and fulfilment through intimate sharing, then we have to take into account the various interlocking levels on which every man and woman lives and which therefore have to be included in that sharing. It's no good, for example, one of the partners taking care to have an excellent sexual rapport with the other, but treating her/his need of feeling appreciated and listened to as of no real importance. And it's no good one partner telling the other that their views are important, but keeping the purse-strings so firmly that those views can have little effect on how the household is run. The physical, the emotional and the financial are all important cylinders in the "motor" of marriage. If any one of them fails to fire, little progress may be made.

The first main danger to a marriage comes from the fact that this rather obvious lesson of common experience is insufficiently considered. A husband or wife can ignore it for years, and have little idea of the suffering that may be being caused and of the damage to the relationship.

It is in this context that can come a subtler and greater danger. It arises from two facts. One of these is, as we've just recalled, that a full relationship between two adults involves relating satisfactorily at several levels. Because of the intimacy, the *emotional* level has a special importance.

Our emotional attitudes begin to be formed, of course, from the beginning of our lives, particularly through our early relationships with our parents. All kinds of family circumstances can lead to some imbalance, such as the long-term absence of a parent. Dr Dominian describes some possible results: "The boy, who remains attached to his mother as he grows up, may find a sexual attraction to women difficult and may marry in order to continue a maternal relationship, and similarly the girl, who idealizes her father or on the contrary never had any closeness with her father, may want a father figure for her husband"[2].

When such people marry, they may not have achieved a clear and confident sense of their own identity. They marry protective or even masterful spouses. And, as their marriages unfold, the paternalistic traits in their spouses are encouraged by the dependent partners themselves. It is, after all, what they feel they need!

The years go by. The couples may have no clear consciousness that there is an imbalance between them. In fact, the insecure partner may even pass as the more masterful. He or she seeks the clear and confident identity which is not available in the relationship through achievement instead. The successes that may result seem to be evidence that there is really no problem.

Then, at some stage, the dependent partner may change. Even as late as the fifties, he or she may achieve a clear sense of identity, emotional independence, and an adequate self-esteem.

The inevitable result is a fundamental change in the "chemistry" of the marriage relationship. Over ten, twenty, or even thirty years, one of the partners has been tacitly required to play the parent-figure. That role not only corresponds, very likely, to some of that partner's character, but it has become ingrained, second-nature, from all those years of use. How possible will it be for this partner to make a profound change in his or her basic approach, perhaps in the forties or fifties, and perhaps at a stage of the marriage which is anyway quite delicate – say, when the couple have to adjust to the recent departure of the now grown-up children, for whom they may have very largely been living?

And, if the parent-figure partner cannot make the change, what will be the situation of the partner who has undergone this change? He or she has at last achieved self-possession: the feeling of being a worth-while, independent person. Can he or she tolerate what may well appear a "life-sentence" of being treated as a child? He or she now experiences the other, not as a needed support, but as a permanent obstacle to what has now become his or her deepest and most urgent emotional need.

This is not to say that the problem cannot be solved. But that is unlikely to happen unless the partners are aware of its nature. Then much will depend on the trust they have built up in each other and the persistence, love and self-sacrifice with which they will work at readjusting to this major new development.

But what is the situation when the couple do not understand what has happened to their relationship (because no one has ever explained it), or when they haven't built up the ability to listen and respond to each other's deeper feelings, even with the help of a counsellor?

Dr Dominian describes what may sometimes be the case: "In some instances it can truly be said that the person who married changes completely in the next few years. Spouses have to adapt to each other's gradual transformations but it is not surprising that such major alterations in identity may be incompatible with the continuation of a marriage"[3].

There are, of course, unfortunately, other kinds of serious imbalances in or between partners that can make it difficult to discern the existence of any real marriage relationship between them. This particular kind has been described because it raises a key question about Catholics and divorce. The Church's present practice is only to dissolve marriages which it finds, after prolonged examination, not to have been a true marriage relationship from the start. But are we now forced to say that what starts as an adequate, if weak, marriage relationship can, perhaps years later, simply go dead? In chapters 5 and 6 we shall see how Catholic theologians and church lawyers are tackling this question.

A Few Conclusions?

From what we've seen so far, we may be inclined to conclude that modern marriage has something in common with a motor car. The car has opened up for innumerable families new horizons of experience – a century ago most of us would hardly ever have left our remote village! Marriage today, like the car, can bring much happiness – of course much more deeply!

But what do we think of a car owner who handles the vehicle carelessly, or doesn't learn at least the basic facts about safe driving? An Australian friend, travelling for the first time in the outback, mentioned in passing that he had just one spare wheel. The people he was visiting expressed horror, with all the bluntness that Australian idiom can command! They had seen so often what could easily be the outcome.

We are all well aware of the likely outcome of a broken marriage. Psychologists tell us that the children's development will be retarded in those important years, and that the long-term effects may possibly be even more serious. In the U.K. today there are a million one-parent families, mainly from divorce, and in the U.S.A. there are twelve million children under the age of eighteen whose parents are divorced. Because the single parent can seem a threat to married couples, a feeling of rejection from them, and of loneliness, can be added to the loss of the former partner.

A car crash – and a divorce – may rightly prompt sympathy, not blame. The people concerned may well have done their best to avoid the tragedy or simply be the victims of circumstance. We know enough about what constitutes an intimate relationship and about the many types and phases of human development to appreciate what the couple may have been through.

But all that seems to lead to three conclusions.

First, an educated couple today who do not make sure that they are aware of the main levels at which they will need to relate, and the difficulties that may arise, are not unlike my Australian friend in the outback.

The second conclusion is that we've never had a greater need of Christ's teaching about marriage and divorce. To tackle the difficulties that arise in many marriages, and to avoid the damage inflicted by divorce, we need authentic and strong motivation. Christ's teaching is uniquely capable of giving us that, especially today, when we are in a much better position to discern its real nature. We shall consider that in the next chapter.

The third conclusion concerns the local Christian community. Especially in this decade, when the contemporary kind of marriage is relatively new and therefore quite frequently not well understood, couples can need help in being able to foresee and forestall any likely crises and to handle them when they arise. Divorced people may feel rejected and need appropriate support. The divorced–remarried may feel alienated and unwanted by the Church.

All these are our brothers and sisters through their

baptism. Without love, we are "nothing" (1 Corinthians 13:2–3). In chapter 9 we shall see some of the ways of serving these people in love that parishes may consider.

2.

The Gospels on Divorce

How do our non-Christian friends view Jesus' prohibition of divorce?

Many see it, I suspect, as a very strict law imposed only on Christians. They may welcome the Christian stand against easy divorce, but they doubt whether an absolute law is an effective way of doing that. When they notice that the proportion of Catholic divorces is no lower than that of the population generally, their doubt naturally becomes even stronger.

But *did* Jesus deal in laws? And *was* his concern simply with his followers? The New Testament, I believe, makes us answer firmly "No". Jesus was doing something much more important than tightening up divorce regulations for those who joined him.

Jesus had come to form for God a new people. The job of this people is to show the whole world what human life is really meant to be. At last all people should be able to see that there *is* a God in the world – a central, creative force of faithful love. And God's presence should be recognized, not from some supernatural revelations given to the few, but from the best evidence of all: true humanity.

"The glory of God is a man or woman fully alive" was the nub of Jesus' aim. His followers are meant to show, through the way they live, what the gift of being human offers to *everyone*.

Because of that, Jesus had little interest in laws and directives. A person "fully alive" isn't programmed by anyone. So Jesus' teaching was not primarily through words, but through the way that he and his followers lived. In that you could see – if you cared to look – the compassion, the joy, the love and the courage, and the fruit that these brought in people's lives. Of course words were used. But instead of telling you what to think, most of them simply told you stories. "Here's a bit of life", Jesus' parables said. "Does it help you understand what you see me doing?" Jesus' teaching appealed to your sense of responsibility: it didn't "programme" you!

The Degradation of Marriage

Life, for virtually all Jews, included marriage. How could Jesus, as unmarried, show his audiences and disciples how a fully human person lived as a man or wife?

His difficulty was immense. The contemporary Jewish attitude to marriage was the major obstacle. It had made people accustomed to several inhuman practices. Jesus had to help his listeners see that these were wrong. Among the most flagrant of those practices was the way they divorced.

For many centuries before Christ, Jewish law had allowed a husband to dismiss his wife unilaterally. The only stipulation was that he had found in her "something indecent". According to one school of thought, this meant that she had to be guilty of serious sexual misconduct. But, according to an equally influential school, virtually any reason would do.

The profound insight in Genesis, that marriage is a

real partnership, had been lost to view. All the power was the husband's. He "acquired" a wife – just as he might acquire a farm or a herd of cattle. And relinquishing "his" wife was just as easy.

This widespread degradation of marriage in Jesus' day was compounded by the more extreme cases. A husband noticed that his meals were regularly unappetizing, or that his wife was less attractive than another woman. Respected legal authorities told him that he could dismiss her. Even bad breath, unkempt hair, or noisy talk in the house that could be heard by the neighbours, counted as valid grounds for divorce. A marriage for a night seemed entirely within the law.

Jesus had to try to turn round this strong tide of old and deepset attitudes. The dignity of women and the very nature of marriage had somehow to be restored.

That Jesus insisted that love and respect are central to any really human life is widely known. But the story of how Jesus – and Paul after him – insisted on the equal dignity of women is now only beginning to be told. The backdrop to that story is also better recognized. It was not just in the matter of divorce, but in every sphere of life, that the Jews – like the Greeks and Romans – regarded women as inferior. It is true that there were exceptions. We know of Jewish women in commerce, and even a reigning Jewish queen. But the general view of them as second-class citizens was deep and unmistakable.

The early Christians were to find that to follow Jesus in opposing that deeply ingrained trend was to court enormous difficulties. A wife was obliged, by the customary marriage contract, to get the permission of her husband before going out alone. What was a Christian wife of a pagan husband to do when she wanted to work among the poor or to join her fellow Christians for worship? – situations where she could take as responsible a part as men? And could she agree to go with her husband on social or business occasions, when food sacrificed to idols would be eaten?

If Christian wives regularly and publicly refused to obey their husbands in such matters, then their neighbours would see this new religion as undermining the very fabric of society, since the health of the state had long been thought to depend on the health of its family life. The Christians had enough persecution on their hands without causing this further provocation. But it was too fundamental to Jesus' teaching for them to abandon it.

When Jesus spoke, all that was, of course, largely in the future. It was a major problem that the early Christian communities would have to confront. But the problems they found themselves facing were symptomatic of the difficulty of anyone, in Jesus' world, in denouncing male dominance. That dominance was not a philosophical fad cherished by some right-wing loonies. It lay at the very heart of the marriage relationship, as it was psychologically experienced by husbands, and as it was officially understood. The wife was a man's possession. She largely ranked with children.

Jesus' Response

Jesus made clear that his stand against all this was fundamental. It was not just a footnote to his programme, and it went much deeper than a prohibition against divorce. That prohibition can be understood only within the framework of what he wanted to say about the marriage relationship itself.

Mark brings this out most clearly when he shows the Pharisees asking Jesus whether "our Law allows a man to divorce his wife" (10:2). Jesus answers their question by going straight to what he saw as the central issue, which was God's original intention for marriage: "how it was from the beginning", as that was then expressed:

> Haven't you read the Scripture that says that *in the beginning* the Creator made people male and female? And God said, "For this reason a man will leave his father and mother and unite with his wife, and the two will become one. So they are no longer two, but one" (Mark 10:6–8).

Jesus uses the method his contemporaries would have recognized, of appealing to a whole passage of Scripture by quoting a small part of it. Here he takes one verse each from the first two chapters of Genesis (1:27; 2:24).

Genesis makes clear that human life was made to be lived as a male-female partnership (2:18): a man is incomplete without a woman; and she is needed as his "partner". That partnership should extend over the whole spectrum of their human experience. That is the first thing that Adam recognizes in Eve: she shared with him in everything: all the way from his "bone" (i.e. his strength) to his "flesh" (i.e. his weakness).

Their partnership was intended to be one of deep love and tenderness. This comes out very strongly in the second verse of Jesus' quotation. It echoes the language the Bible uses elsewhere about God's relationship (his "covenant") with his own dear people. God's purpose in that was not to dominate but to serve. It was founded on faithful love and complete sharing.

Genesis goes on to emphasize the completeness of marriage's sharing. When it says that "the two of them become one body" (2:24), it means much more than sexual intercourse, though it certainly includes that. They share in life's adventure together, with an increasingly common purpose.

So marriage is not a deal where you acquire a potentially tiresome possession and ask when you might lawfully get rid of it if it turns out not to suit you. It is an opportunity to move from the deadness of self-centredness to appreciating and loving the humanity of another person. Only if you do that, and do it wholeheartedly, are you fully alive. Only in that way do you plunge into the adventure of life with your whole self – feelings, sexuality, mind and will – to heal and build and bring to great fruitfulness.

Many scholars believe that what Mark is giving us here is an early Christian community's writing up of Jesus' teaching on divorce and marriage. If so, that anonymous community did a remarkably good job, as we see when we turn to Jesus' direct statements on divorce.

When we look at those statements, our first impression may be of some confusion. As on many other central matters – like Jesus' parables and his Last Supper – each gospel writer responds to the situation of his audience, decades after Jesus' death, by feeling free to retouch an earlier version. But it is possible to peel off the gospel writers' adaptations and reach back to

Jesus' actual words with a good deal of probability. What we find, when we do so, is something very different from our contemporary expectation.

First, we find that they are much more about marriage than divorce. The two almost certainly authentic statements are:

> "Man must not separate what God has joined together."
> "Whoever dismisses his wife commits adultery, and whoever marries the dismissed wife commits adultery."

The first is one of those lapidary appeals to God's original intention that are typical of Jesus. It is a radical indictment of the views of a Jewish audience. "You think", it says to Jesus' audience, "that married life consists of a man 'taking' a woman. As a result, in your marriage ceremony, only the man makes the contract. And you understand divorce as a man undoing what he himself has done: he gets rid of one of his 'possessions'."

"What you've forgotten is God! This whole creation is *God's* – and yours. You were to be like God and therefore lords over the world (Genesis 1:27). But you can do so only if you live up to your vocation of *becoming full human beings*. Marriage is, for most of you, your greatest opportunity of doing that. There your humanity can come to great fulfilment. But the very reverse of that happens if you treat your partner as a chattel. If you remembered how marriage is part of God's strategy for your own enrichment as human persons, your men could not dismiss their wives in that way."

Jesus' other saying on divorce is even more clearly focused on the Jewish attitude to marriage: "Whoever dismisses his wife commits adultery, and whoever marries the dismissed wife commits adultery." *We* may regard this as a general law about divorce, although a bit more obscure than we would have wished. But to Jesus' audience, it was neither a law nor obscure. It was the clearest possible *demand for a radical revision of their beliefs about adultery and marriage*.

Adultery, for the Jews, consisted in infringing *the husband's* (never the wife's) property rights, his rights over his wife. A husband could have as many affairs with unmarried women as he liked without committing adultery. And, if he slept with a married woman, that was adulterous *not* because it was a wrongful infringement of his married relationship (viz. adultery), but because it infringed the property rights of his mistress's husband!

Jesus' statement is insisting that marriage is not a matter of property rights but of a total commitment, in love, between two people. To dismiss your spouse as you would a slave or other possession *is* adultery because it arises from a subhuman practice of marriage. Anyone who understood and lived the kind of marriage for which, as human beings, we were intended, could never do that.

The same kind of reasoning is being applied in the second half of Jesus' statement. A man marrying a wife dismissed in that way is conniving at marriage being demeaned in that way. By the Jews' beliefs about marriage, he was acting within his rights. "No!" Jesus is saying. "He is a marriage-destroyer: an adulterer."

Laws? Or More?

Jesus' statements above divorce are usually considered to be laws. People scrutinize them, weighing every word, like lawyers. But by looking at their original intention, we see that they are both more than that – and less!

Consider what happens when I break a law. Say that I deduct ten per cent from my tax payments because I can't morally approve of ten per cent of state expenditure. The law forbids me to do that, so it can punish me. The law will not tell me that, by refusing to pay the tax, *I am damaging myself*, my integrity as a human being. It does not, in other words, make a *moral* comment. All it says is that if I don't pay it, *the state will "damage" me*. In this matter, it insists on taking my moral decisions for me.

The overwhelming consensus of Scripture scholars believes that Jesus' statements on divorce were intended to be understood very differently, and precisely in the two characteristics of law we've just noted.

1. Unlike the Law, Jesus *was* making a moral comment. He *was* telling us that if we act in those ways we do great damage to ourselves, in the most valuable of our possessions: our own human integrity. His statements are not arbitrary or strict rules that God happens to impose, but indications of what is involved in being human.

2. Unlike the Law, Jesus was *not* taking our moral decision for us. As in the rest of Jesus' teaching, he was asking us to take another look at ourselves and our opportunities, and the damage we can do. Jesus always appealed to and encouraged our sense of responsibility; he never overrode it.

This new insight naturally has very important practical consequences, which we must start to explore. Because the insight is quite new, and so much is at stake, our exploration will need to be a careful one. We can, nevertheless, have confidence that we are setting out in the right direction. Scripture scholars differ on many things; but on Jesus' statements *not* being laws, there is massive agreement[4]. They feel forced to this conclusion not only by Jesus' insistence on people's responsibility and freedom, but also because St Paul, as we shall see, felt obliged to approve of divorce when that seemed to be demanded by the claims of other important Christian values.

The common conclusion of Scripture scholars on this matter has been spelt out by one writer:

> In the matter of divorce, as with other questions in Christian ethics, one cannot obtain from the New Testament a universally applicable rule, but each Christian must, in each particular situation, examine, in the light of what the New Testament shows, what God's will is in these specific circumstances. He or she can only succeed through exercising their own responsibility before God[5].

Christians should make use of this insight *as a member of Christ's Church*. For us to live as though we do not need to give and receive from the other members is as unnatural and self-defeating, Paul says, as an eye saying to the hand "I have no need of you"! (1 Corinthians 12:21). Each must make his or her own decisions; but we are called to form our moral values together.

35

This was beautifully expressed by an outstanding Catholic Scripture scholar:

> Jesus' ethic is not directed to isolated individuals, but to the circle of disciples, the new family of God, the people of God which is to be gathered. Whether or not this ethic can be fulfilled is something that can only be determined by groups of people . . . [who] wish to be real communities of brothers and sisters – communities which form a living arena for faith, in which everyone draws strength from each other[6].

3.

St Paul on Divorce

Our concern so far has been with Jesus' own teaching.
By turning our attention now to Paul, we see how that
teaching was understood and applied by the only New
Testament writer to repeat Jesus' teaching on divorce.
That is not only the best way of checking the accuracy
of the interpretation we have given, but it will also
greatly help us in the rest of the book when we apply
Jesus' teaching to our situation today.

Crazy Notions in Corinth

Paul, it is true, has had a bad press on the matter of
marriage. He is widely thought of as anti-women and
anti-marriage. But even criminals are usually tried in
the light of the evidence! To that we must now turn.

Paul, like Jesus, deals with divorce in the context of
problems about sex and marriage. He was writing to
the Christians at Corinth about twenty-four years
after Jesus' death. He knew, from long experience, that
they were marvellous at getting things wrong. On these
two topics they certainly lived up to that reputation!

Just before the part of the letter in which Paul deals
with divorce (1 Corinthians 7:10–16), Paul has been
trying to correct two major misunderstandings
(6:12–7:6). The Corinthians had come to believe that
the body no longer mattered. They were now con-

vinced that they already *had* salvation. Since their baptism had promoted them to the level of the "spiritual", physical things like bodies and sex were at best irrelevant and at worst degrading. They were childish things. As Christian adults, they could no longer take them seriously.

About the practical conclusions they should draw from that, their opinions differed. Some concluded that a Christian could sleep with anyone – bodies were too unimportant to be capable of sin. Others concluded that to have sex at all was degrading. It sucked you down to the level of the "merely" physical. We may regard such notions as too idiotic to spend time on; but Paul, as these people's leader, had to take them seriously. He either knew, or could guess, the devastating effects they would be having on people.

First, it was making them into spiritual "prima donnas". Their attention was focused on their own spiritual achievements, not on Christ's loving presence in them, from which alone their strength could come.

Love of their fellow Christians was another casualty, as pride in their "spiritual" achievements, rivalry and self-centredness took centre stage in their lives.

The most fundamental damage was to their belief in the resurrection of themselves as physical people: the "good news" on which all Christianity is founded (15:1–19).

The most obvious effects of their contempt of the physical were of course in the matter of their sexual relationships. Those who deduced from that contempt that they could sleep with whom they pleased were bringing Christian values into disrepute. And those who took the view that sexual intercourse is bad for a

Christian and should therefore be avoided were likely to put an intolerable strain on their marriage partner.

Paul's View of Marriage

Paul's answer stresses the central importance of our bodies, including our sexuality, in our Christian lives. God will raise us *as physical beings*, just as he did Christ (6:13–14). Our vocation as Christ's "body" is to be a physically visible sign to the world of his love and his presence. And then Paul quotes some of the words that we saw Jesus take from Genesis when he wanted to underline the enormous value of sex in the marriage relationship (Genesis 2:24).

Paul, in other words, saw the physical side of our nature as an indispensable and potentially very fruitful element in every Christian's life. He therefore attached great importance to sexuality and marriage. So strongly was that the case, that when we look at him tackling problems concerning them, we find his views on them were revolutionary! Before his conversion, his beliefs about the role of women would, like any Pharisee's, have been most conservative. His Christianity had evidently forced him to appreciate, nineteen centuries before our time, that in marriage the love, respect and obligations should be mutual. Each must respond to the other as equal in human dignity (7:2–4, 10–16). Neither Jews nor Greeks even approached making that demand.

Paul's View on Divorce

All this helps us to appreciate what Paul is talking about when he discusses in this chapter the termination of marriages. He believed that a marriage relationship, by its

very nature, should be *a richly human way of life*.
Besides the evidence we've already seen, we have his
treatment of divorce later in this chapter. There he
implicitly accepts the view that a marriage in which at
least one partner is a Christian needs to have an
atmosphere where the kind of values he has been
talking about can, realistically, be nurtured. Paul
thought about marriage not as an abstract ideal, but
always as a lived reality.

His first task in the chapter is to try to correct the
married people who had been led, by their spiritual
snobbery, to refrain from intercourse. Their slogan
was: "It's wrong for a man to have sexual intercourse
with a woman" (7:1)**. Paul's reply is: "That's
robbery!" (7:5). "It's refusing to give your partner what
you owe to him/her" – not just the right to sex, but also
the right to care and love (7:3).

But Paul was in Ephesus; and he knew that the
letters between Corinth and himself would take several
weeks. The help he was now offering might not arrive
before some marriages had reached breaking point, or
even gone beyond it.

This may help to clear up our difficulties about Paul's
first statement about divorce (7:10–11). We have
always to remember in reading Paul that we're listening
in to only one side of a conversation. The situation
being discussed was known by both parties and didn't
need spelling out. For us to understand what Paul is
saying often involves some detective work.

The most probable reconstruction of what is going on

** In this chapter, double asterisks mean that the translation of text
has been amended in the light of the findings of modern
scholarship.

in this section starts with the Corinthian slogan that "It is wrong for a man to have sexual intercourse with a woman". Some Corinthian Christian men (at least) were living by this belief. Their wives' claims of their rights became increasingly irksome. These men at length concluded that their marriages had no future. Dismissing their wives was the only way to preserve their "superior" kind of Christian life!

Paul has already abundantly tried to show these people that their reasoning was wrong. If logic were all, he had no need to do more than spell out the practical application to their problem of his treatment of Christian marriage. Almost all his answer in fact does that: "The woman should not allow herself to be divorced – but if (by the time my letter reaches you) that has already happened, she should remain de-married or be reconciled to her husband. And the man should not divorce his wife"**. In other words: "Sort out your attitudes to marriage in the light of what I've said. Don't rush into any precipitate action (like remarriage) if you've already got divorced. Your aim should be a better grasp of the truth, and reconciliation between you."

The important question for our purposes is: on what grounds does Paul say this? From the way he introduces this instruction, the grounds are clearly twofold. The first is all he had been saying about marriage and divorce. Then, just as he is about to apply that, he remembers Jesus' prohibition of divorce; and then he bases this instruction on that. "To the married I enjoin you – or rather, not me, but the Lord. . . ."

Is Paul suggesting that Jesus' prohibition settles *all* divorce matters – at least for Christians – so that his earlier discussion about what marriage is supposed to be becomes irrelevant to that? In other words, is Jesus' prohibition of divorce the *only* determining factor, so that all divorce, for Christians, is forbidden? Or is it *one* determining factor, along with the nature of Christian marriage and the nature of a couple's relationship?

In answering that question, we will want to bear in mind what we already know:

1. Jesus didn't promulgate a law about divorce, but a fundamental insight into the nature of any true marriage relationship.

2. In other matters, Paul himself took Jesus' directives very seriously *as indications of important Christian values*. But if, in a given situation, a more important Christian value was at stake and both could not be had, then he would consider himself obliged to follow the latter (cf 1 Corinthians 9:1–23).

3. As we shall see in a moment, Paul *did* allow divorce in certain circumstances. This is additional evidence that Jesus' prohibition did not, for Paul, apply to all marriages. Some would reply to that: "It applied at least to all marriages where both partners are Christians."

So far as *Jesus himself* was concerned, this was certainly not true. First, he was talking to Jews, not to Christians. And, more importantly, his whole argument rested on what God wanted for all people because of the nature he had given them.

So far as *Paul* is concerned, it is certainly true that Paul mentions the prohibition only when dealing with marriage between Christians. But, if he understood it as one vital insight and not as an ill-determining law, he did not need to mention it again when he dealt with the "mixed marriage" case (which we'll come to in a moment). His letter is already by far his longest. He can only devote a few lines to most of the many problems he has to deal with, and therefore quickly alludes to the most decisive issues in each. In the case of *the two Christian partners*, the issues consisted of some aspects of the true nature of marriage and the Lord's prohibition. In the *"mixed marriage" case*, the decisive issue was another vital aspect of a marriage. Like Jesus he saw the prohibition as being intended to throw most important light on *all* marriages – not just Christian ones. But he had no reason to think that it was intended to be the *only* light.

"Let There Be a Divorce" (7:12–16)

The other case on which Paul had to comment was very different from the first. Two pagans had married some time ago; and then one of them had become a Christian. Corinth was like many a sea-port then and now: full of a largely rootless population, prone to immoral values. One of those values, we've already seen, was spiritual rivalry and its attendant self-centredness. Even some of the leading Christians were much more interested in taking the temperature of their own spiritual health than in following Jesus' one "law" of practical, loving service (cf Galatians 6:2).

Having a pagan marriage partner could easily be seen by such people as a threat to that "health". There would be deep differences of views and values, and probably major clashes. Was this really the kind of atmosphere in which one's new-found Christian faith could flourish?

Paul's answer is "Yes! It often can be! Marriage is not about selfish satisfaction. It's about healing and sustaining one another so that both of you can grow as people. In a word, it's about mutual loving service. By gently persisting with your Christian values, you may gradually commend them to your partner. You create a Christian atmosphere. The path to that may be rough – but Christian life, and even most marriages, are not immune to considerable difficulties. But look what you may achieve: you will have made it possible for your partner to be 'holy'!" The pagan partner, in other words, could be helped to touch the summit of human achievement: the purpose of God's whole plan. "This is God's design for you," Paul had told the Thessalonians, "your holiness" (1 Thessalonians 4:3).

Paul was deeply opposed, we see from that, to "easy" divorce. For a Christian to call the lawyer after a few big rows would have seemed to him a gross betrayal of any marriage, and particularly a Christian one. But at the same time he believed that Christianity is about taking human reality very seriously. That is what Christ had embraced. And that is what Christians are called to transform. One bit of human reality is the sadness of an impossible marriage. "If the one who is not a believer wishes to be divorced, let there be a divorce. God has called you to live in peace" (7:15)**. The profound insight that Jesus' pro-hibition had voiced remained of great importance. But in this case, a higher value transcended it: "God has called you to live in peace." And – as if to emphasize that *all* relevant human values must be responsibly weighed: "How (in such a case) do you know whether you will save your spouse?" (7:16)**.

Summing up Part 1

In these three chapters we have been assembling the data we need in order to enter into the present reflection on divorce in the Church. In the rest of the book, we shall be considering the consequences that Catholic theologians and lawyers are already beginning to draw from this data. It may be helpful, before we do that, to sum up briefly what that is:

1. There is a very serious divorce problem in the countries of the Western world. Much unhappiness, and damage to children, results. This must be understood in the context of marriage as it is lived today.

2. Most people expect much more from marriage than did earlier generations. Such expectations are often fulfilled to a large degree. But they, and the much greater length of most married lives, help to make marriage more vulnerable. This is particularly true if a couple don't really try to share at the various levels at which we all live, especially the emotional level; or if there is a very considerable late development of one partner at the emotional level to which the other partner can't adequately adapt.

3. The purpose of the Church is *to serve the world* (not primarily Christians) by showing it, through the life of Christ in us, truly human life. This is what we must show in the married lives of Christians, and in how we handle the breakdown and difficulties of Christian marriages.

4. When Jesus spoke about divorce, he was trying to help his Jewish audience to understand what God in-

tended for any human marriage. He naturally did this in terms of their own understanding and practice in regard to marriage. A truly human marriage involved *not* treating your partner as an object or a possession, but as an equal with whom you happily shared your common experience of life's adventure. Taking the initiative in dismissing your partner conflicted fundamentally with that.

5. Virtually all Scripture scholars, Catholic and otherwise, agree that Jesus' statements on divorce are not seen by the New Testament to be taken as laws.

6. Jesus did not deal explicitly with two questions that concern us: (a) What is the situation if your partner divorces you? (b) What should you do if your marriage really "dies": i.e. you can no longer relate as partners? These questions were not major problems in Jesus' time.

7. Paul also spoke about divorce in the context of marriage. Like Jesus, too, he does not give us a full treatment of divorce questions. He tells a couple where one partner has false ideas about sex, to seek reconciliation. Christian spouses married to non-believers are to shoulder their difficulties in a constructive way and not to seek divorce. But if the non-believer seeks a divorce, that is to be allowed, because God's having called us to peace then takes precedence over Jesus' prohibition.

8. Jesus had not explicitly said that it is wrong to accept divorce if your partner divorces you; and Paul said that at least in one kind of case it was right to do so. Theologians, as we shall see, ask whether Paul would not have come to the same conclusion in similar cases of one spouse being abandoned by the other.

PART 2

Consequences

4.

Enter the Laity

"It is essential for the Church to question itself again and again to make sure if it is doing justice to people in all the difficult and complex situations in which they find themselves in the modern world or whether it is not helping them in those situations"[7]. This quotation, from a major Catholic theologian writing about divorce, describes the purpose of this book. We want to make sure that we, the Church, are doing justice to our fellow Catholics "in all the difficult and complex situations in which they find themselves" in the matter of divorce.

It is because we realize that all mature Catholics have a responsibility in this matter that we have been sifting the evidence. Bishops at the Roman Synod on the Family in 1980 made it plain that married people have a major role in this enquiry. Another Catholic theologian points to the basic reason:

What do we look for when we turn to the New Testament and the teaching of Jesus? Do we seek the formulation of an absolute, divinely revealed law or model, or do we seek a process of understanding and adaptation with which the modern Church can identify by entering into the process and furthering it? I believe it is the latter that is the more appropriate by virtue of the nature of the New

49

Testament materials themselves. The Church of today must relate, not to an absolute divine law which is in practice inaccessible to our scholarly research, but to the process of identifying what is of Christ and what is Christian and entering into that discerning process for our own day. The matrix of modern discernment is, as it was in the churches of Paul or Matthew, the dwelling of the Holy Spirit among God's people[8].

If we accept that as valid, we shall look for the answers not in our individual wisdoms, but in the prayerful discernment in God's people. We will be open to the Spirit and to the experience and insights – however tentative – of each other. And we will be aware of the responsibility that is ours – helping to form the Church's stance to millions of divorced Catholics and its ministry of love and understanding to them.

In the rest of this book we shall enter into the discussion by Catholics about divorce in that spirit. That discussion, we have seen, has arisen from today's fuller understanding of the Scripture evidence and of the psychological realities of many marriages. It is asking such questions as: Could divorce, in some circumstances, be allowed for Catholics? Should divorced and remarried Catholics be denied the Eucharist? Are the Church courts which deal with requests for "annulments" operating on the right principles?

These are questions that have been asked by theologians and bishops, with mounting insistence, for over a decade. Now that we have examined the data on which those questions are based, we can accept the request of Church leaders and enter into the debate.

We will want to bear in mind, throughout, the great responsibility of the task to which we have been invited. What is required is to do full justice *both* to what Christ said about marriage and divorce *and* to the situation of Christian couples.

This is our task, not as mere individuals, but *as members of the Church*. If we "go it alone" we turn our backs on Christ's "body", in whom his Spirit of truth dwells.

The success of a debate depends quite largely on the spirit in which it is conducted. Because we are looking for wisdom – not quick answers – as members of the Church, we want to seek this in the spirit described long ago by Gregory Baum:

We want to be faithful to the teaching authority of the Church. We realize that wisdom is given by God to the community. As we are dependent on others for love, so we are dependent on others for truth. For this reason, the Catholic theologian has learned to profess his positions in a tentative way, as questions, as contributions to dialogue, and he refuses to engage himself wholeheartedly in his own convictions unless he knows himself to be accompanied by the brethren, that is the Church[9].

5.

Catholic Thinking on Divorce Today

We saw earlier in this book that when a couple get married today, their situation and their aims are likely to be rather different from that of their grandparents. Mutual love, for instance, is more likely to be at the forefront of their aims, and there will be far less support for the permanence of their relationship than previously.

Two decades ago, this would not have triggered off a debate among Catholics about divorce. A marriage between Catholics was permanent – except for some arcane exceptions. Catholic teaching said so. Any assertion that the realities of the contemporary situation are centrally relevant to official Catholic teaching and practice about divorce would have been universally rejected.

It was not until the 1960s that it was officially recognized that the New Testament pointed decisively in a very different direction. Christ did not set up an unchangeable system and then tell us somehow to fit into it. He began, not with a system, but with people. The one aim was that, in the reality of people's lives – first, in his own, and then in those of Christians – God's loving, creative presence could be known and appreciated.

The lives of married couples were potentially one of the strongest signs of that presence. There you could see a couple being gradually transformed by the example and presence of Christ into people who showed the fruit of the Spirit in life as we live it: its ordinariness, its pleasure and its pain, its strength and weakness. In the lives of couples and their families, God's warm, creative presence could be *seen* and *felt*: the way we, as human, relate to things. God was expressing himself there in human language, just as he did in the very human life of Christ.

"Not me! I'm just an ordinary person!" is likely to be our incredulous reaction. Surely God is above us, different from us. But if we look at Genesis, we see that the vocation of all men and women is precisely that: to be "the human projection" – the "sacrament" of God (1:27).

The point of Christ's life, and now of ours as Christians, is to show how that can be. We know that can't be a walk-over. We are aware of human sinfulness: that this will often be going against the grain: that a certain "militancy" will be necessary.

We also know that this business of being God's "sacrament" is not, as we used to suppose, something we do mainly in church, but what we're called to be and to do for our world as Christ did for his.

So the practical question is: How can our kind of married life today realistically make God's creative presence seen and felt and loved? How, in other words, can the married lives of Christian couples be more fully a Christian sacrament? What attitudes and practices may we have to change or strengthen to achieve that? This is what the current debate about divorce is concerned with.

Today's New Priorities

We began our enquiry with Allison being asked to be a "*first wife*". That *New Yorker* cartoon is true to the extent that people's confidence in the possibility of lasting fidelity in married life has been greatly diminished. Never has there been a greater need of *persuasive* examples of that.

The debate therefore starts with a careful look at the forces in our society that are undermining that. What is making fidelity in marriage much more difficult to attain?

> In other times, family life and fidelity had priority in mind, myth, and social imagination. . . .What took their place as top priority was work in the public marketplace rewarded by freedom and the celebration of individualistic pleasure in one's private life. The hero moved from the hearth to the professional suite[10].

This focus on work outside the family and on individualistic pleasure has come at a time when the barriers that used to stand against divorce have disintegrated. Many countries, for example, provide easy, cheap divorce, and the social expectations of the neighbourhood no longer oppose it. We are therefore faced with the fact that the current divorce attitudes and practices arise from deeply-ingrained tendencies in our kind of world.

The Church's Response

1 *Our responsibility to the world*

The first consequence is to confirm the importance of the Christian responsibility in this matter. "The Church is, after all, almost the only relevant reality in society today that has the moral authority to represent this fundamentally Christian faithfulness in marriage".[11]

But how exactly can we fulfil this role? If the vocation of Christian married couples is to show the world what marriage can be like, how best can they do that in cases where there is a breakdown of marriage? And we may like to remind ourselves that we are talking here not only of a great number of human tragedies, but also of what the world will rightly regard to be a test case of whether the Church does stand for true humanity.

One place from which to start trying to answer our question is the one chosen by many bishops at the Roman Synod on the Family in 1980. The French bishops, for example, had prepared for the Synod by distributing a questionnaire throughout France. The majority of the fifty thousand people who replied believed that Catholic morality with regard to the divorced and remarried had lost touch with the realities of everyday life. Their request to their bishops was: "Please don't bury our questions."

This sense of remoteness from reality was certainly not confined to France. In a restrained book on Christian marriage in 1977, one of the best Catholic theologians of Germany had said that "many practising Christians find the Church's teaching [on sexuality and marriage] if not hostile to life, then at least very remote from life today"[12]. And a distinguished American theologian was asking, in 1980, whether there is not "a serious danger that an intransigent interpretation of the indissolubility of marriage in the Catholic Church is rapidly approaching the point of disdain for the ideal itself as a utopian one"[13].

Neither the bishops nor the theologians, were in the least questioning either the truth or the importance of Jesus' teaching about the indissolubility of marriage. They were pointing to the urgency of interpreting it anew in the light of today's valid insights into Scripture, marriage and sexuality.

By asking for this to be done, they were simply being true to the original understanding – recently restored – of sacrament. It's no good our recapturing the awareness that the purpose of a married life is to *show* God – be a sacrament of God – if we don't make sure that it in fact does so! That involves our ensuring that there is a correspondence between *the sign* (our marriages) and *what they're meant to signify* (the loving presence of God). If a funeral or a party means a lot to me, I will take trouble to check that a particular set of clothes will signify my respect and sympathy at the one, or my sharing in a happy occasion at the other. And what we're concerned with in Christian marriage is most of our neighbours' main chance to see that love and meaning will have the last word over selfishness and chaos: that life is basically *for* us: that there is a God in this world.

A Common Example

Let's recall one way in which divorce often happens. A couple start their marriage with the very best of intentions. Then, after some time, things start to go seriously wrong between them. Perhaps one or both of them is seriously at fault. Or perhaps they find themselves faced with difficulties they don't know how to handle. In one way or the other, one eventually decides to finish the marriage and leaves the other partner.

In cases of this kind, what are people – including Catholics – to make of the abandoned partner being forced by the Church into a life of permanent celibacy? Will Scriptual and modern insights lead them to say: "Here is persuasive evidence of the value of Christ's insight into marriage and divorce", or will it lead them to doubt or even deny the validity of that insight?

To answer those questions, and to see where some Catholics' answers would lead us, we may like to take account of some relevant factors.

One factor is Scriptural. In the Genesis insight to which Jesus referred, "humanity as such does not exist. It exists only as man and woman. It is only in togetherness that human existence can be fulfilled in the fully human sense"[14].

In St Paul a life of celibacy was very strongly encouraged. But Paul nevertheless stressed that it was only for those who had been given that special "gift" or charism (1 Corinthians 7:7,17). He was deeply opposed to someone without that gift embracing that vocation.

These Scriptural insights correspond to modern perceptions. Most people are made for the life and companionship of marriage expressed and strengthened by sexual intercourse. A Church that permanently deprives someone of that because he or she has been abandoned by their married partner seems even to many Catholics to *deny* – not to show forth or be a sacrament of – the God of love.

It might seem from this that we've reached an impasse because neither of the two routes before us is acceptable to us as Christians. One route would be to reject the teaching about the indissolubility of marriage. But Christ clearly taught it, so we can't go *that* way.

The other route, of continuing to demand that abandoned spouses never re-marry, would seem to lead us into conflicting with some major Scriptural insights about sexuality as well as major advances in our understanding of men and women. It would therefore gravely damage the possibility of Christian marriage being a sacrament in our time. So, both ways seem barred to us.

But a mechanic who tries to mend this year's engine with last year's implements can find success elusive! Some theologians tell us that we're tackling the problem of divorce with some superseded notions about marriage, sexuality, and, indeed, indissolubility. What understanding of these things do they offer us? Can we accept them? And do they rescue us from our impasse?

Contemporary Christian Insights

1 *About marriage*

It is certainly true that in 1965 the bishops of the Church proclaimed at the Vatican Council a radically developed understanding of marriage. Until they proclaimed this, the Church's official view of marriage had largely neglected love and mutual sharing. The main focus had been on mutually transferring the right to the sexual act.

Take Bill and Jane. When they married they hadn't known each other long enough to be sure whether they could really love each other. At the different levels at which they would need to relate, there was much incompatibility, which they might be able to conquer. But as long as they had freely decided to give each other exclusive sexual rights, then by the official Catholic understanding of marriage prior to 1965, there was certainly a marriage. If they were both Christians, that mutual transference meant that their relationship was a sacrament: it was permanently set to show forth God's loving fidelity to the world. When they had consummated their marriage (i.e. exercised the right they had given to each other), the contract between them had been completed. Since Jesus had said that this contract, marriage, is indissoluble, a completed marriage could not be dissolved. Therefore no one could now dissolve Bill and Jane's marriage. We notice that that logic depends on the marriage being understood as *a contract to give sexual rights*. On the basis of that understanding, it was obvious that the first exercise of sexual intercourse completed the marriage.

But does that logic remain in force now that the bishops and the Pope, at a Council of the Church, have described marriage not as a contract about sexual rights, but as consisting of a relationship of love and sharing?

We can go back to Bill and Jane. Under the old understanding, their freely deciding to give each other such rights meant that they were now married, even if their friends could see that there was little chance of real love in their relationship and that they were probably too incompatible with each other for any deep and lasting sharing. But if, as the bishops and Pope said – and Jesus and Paul before them – love and sharing are central to marriage, *are* Bill and Jane really married? Are they *capable* of marriage with each other?

Once *those* are the realities that make a marriage – not

just the right to sex – it is much more difficult to accept that a very soluble-looking union like this couple's really becomes indissoluble simply because they have fulfilled their promise to give each other exclusive rights to sexual intercourse. We can better see what conclusions are being deduced from this when we've considered sexuality and indissolubility more directly.

2 *About sexuality*

Christians, of course, accept that a central factor in a marriage is giving each other exclusive rights to sexual intercourse. What is new is that psychology has enabled us to understand much better the human reality to which that refers.

Until recently, the official Catholic understanding of the role of sexuality in marriage was that it was for the procreation of children. Catholic psychologists and theologians today would obviously not wish to question that that is a major role. What is now clear is that it isn't the *only* major role. Dr Dominian, for example, lists the following roles that sexual intercourse can have in a marriage:

- a means of *thanksgiving*, not only for the act the couple have just experienced, but for their mutual presence.
- a means of *reassuring* each other that they are wanted and appreciated and that each will be true to the other.
- a means of *reconciliation*.
- a means of *acknowledging* and *reinforcing* each other's sexual identity and personhood.

- a means through which *sustaining*, *healing* and *growth* are affirmed[15].

Because these are its roles, Dominian can call sexual intercourse in marriage "a life-giving encounter"[16]. "Life" here is obviously not confined to the merely physical. It embraces the whole spectrum of intimate human sharing. Sex, in other words, has been profoundly humanized.

Official church teaching seems to be moving surely, if haltingly, in the same direction. What happens if we turn, with this in hand, to our traditional understanding of indissolubility? It says that, in marriage, a couple give each other exclusive rights to sexual intercourse and that on the actual conferring of them the "contract" is completed and therefore indissoluble.

But what about Bill and Jane? They have freely decided to get married – not really for love, but perhaps for plenty of socially acceptable reasons. They wanted children, and they consummated their marriage. But their lack of love and their incompatibility meant that they largely remained like "random isolates bumping into each other". Their sexual intercourse could be pleasurable, but could not be called "life-giving" in the ways just described.

Have Bill and Jane really conveyed to each other the right to *human* sexual intercourse in any full sense of that word? If not, has their "contract" been completed so that it can be called indissoluble?

3 *About indissolubility*

The traditional understanding is well known: Catholic marriages are indissoluble; couples are therefore always obliged to remain together; by doing so they show God's fidelity.

No informed Christian could doubt, I believe, the need of the world to have access to lived examples of God's fidelity – but it must be *God's* kind of fidelity: arising from deep love and intimacy. From the beginning of the Old Testament story and throughout the New Testament, the characteristics most centrally found in God were loving kindness and faithfulness (see especially John 1:14; Exodus 33:12–34:8).

Especially because of the rootlessness and the stress on instant gratification that are so common today, people need *lived evidence* that such a God lives and can be joined and embraced in our world. No testimony to that is more moving and persuasive than the faithful love between Christian couples.

We may think particularly, here, of marriages we've known where considerable difficulties arose and perhaps still persist. It might be of tolerance and understanding that a friend of ours shows for his or her spouse. When you get home from work at the end of a long day and have to cope with a spouse who lives at a different tempo and has different emotional needs, that can grate on you. You need self-control and sympathy, loyalty and love. And you have to persist over days, weeks and years.

That is the reality – and the eloquence – of much faithful sharing. It's not a house you take over ready-made on your marriage day, but something you have to

build brick by brick, even when you'd often much
rather forget all about this "sharing business" and just
slump in front of a television set and shut out from your
mind the need of your partner for help or for signs of
affection.

The difficulty that theologians find with the
traditional Catholic argument about fidelity and indissolubility is *not* in the belief that Catholic marriages –
even those with many "difficulties" – should and often
do show such things. What they question is whether
every Catholic couple, just because they have fulfilled
the requirement of the official teaching of having freely
got married, can then *automatically* be expected to
show loving, life-long fidelity. Have we, in other words,
the right to regard that kind of fidelity as a ready-made
house that you occupy from your marriage day, or is
marriage a very serious commitment to do your best to
build it brick by brick (for example, by the fact that you
don't normally just slump in front of a television set,
however much you may long to do so)? If the second
alternative is true, then it is impossible to exclude the
possibility that your quest may fail. Indissolubility, in
other words, may not be achieved.

These theologians are not at all suggesting that
couples with serious marriage difficulties would be right
to conclude that their efforts to build or deepen their
fidelity are necessarily doomed and that they should
therefore divorce. This would flagrantly ignore facts.
There is the fact of the couple's commitment, itself
sacramental. There is the fact that perhaps most suc-
cessful marriages do run through periods of great
strain. And there is the fact that a person who takes
easy options in that kind of matter obviously becomes

to some extent an "impoverished" human being – as well as an "impoverished" kind of parent.

Their contention, instead, is this. Some marriages, after prolonged effort, do fail. Loving faithfulness between the couple is not achieved, and in some cases never could have been. In such cases, the sacramental *purpose* of indissolubility has vanished; since it is not, and cannot, show forth the loving faithfulness of God. And that obliges them to ask two questions.

The chief question is, of course: does indissolubility in such cases persist? What in Christ's teaching would lead us to believe that to insist on indissolubility when irrevocably deprived of its purpose of showing fidelity would not be like continuing to apply a life-supporting machine to a clearly dead person? And what kind of *sacrament* would that be!

The second question follows from the first. Should we say that not only are we *not entitled* to believe that indissolubility persists in such cases, but also that we are *wrong* to demand it?

What lies behind this second question is, again, our renewed understanding of sacrament and our observation of some marriages. Couples do stay together when they have found they are incapable of a loving relationship with each other. They may find it more convenient, or feel that family or friends expect or need it of them. All that can be fine. Given their circumstances and their responsibilities, it may well be the best arrangement. The question is whether it is really consistent with the Church's own understanding of marriage to *insist* that the couple remain together on the grounds that their marriage is an indissoluble sacrament.

What is it a sacrament *of*? Is what has irrevocably become a cold or remote relationship a sign of God's loving faithfulness? Would insisting that this relationship is a sacrament not only be a wrong to the couple but also a counter-sign to the world?

For the world will deduce that one feature of Christian marriage is forcing couples to remain for life bound in a loveless marriage, not simply because of their responsibilities to each other or the children, but *in the name of the Christian understanding of marriage*.

That, then, is the basic argument. It is wrong to force all couples to remain together, whatever their circumstances, simply on the grounds that they have a duty to show fidelity and that *by remaining together they could do so*. These theologians are saying that some couples cannot show anything but a kind of fidelity unworthy of the name, by remaining together. Where that is *genuinely* the case – and they grant that self-deception is very easy in the matter – they suggest that the reason for any such insistence collapses.

Here, as with marriage and sexuality, we are considering a very recent development in understanding, and therefore a new issue. We saw in chapter 1 that until the present century fidelity in marriage was, for most people, no great problem. Since there were quite widely no high expectations of love, a cold relationship was likely to pass in most cases for faithfulness. The circumstances of work and the neighbourhood encouraged couples to stay as husband and wife within that context.

Our own situation is obviously very different. Professor Aubert, who has been writing for many years on this question, summed it up succinctly: "Today fidelity is no longer inscribed in the social and economic structure as a given from the beginning. It can only be a task, a goal to pursue. And it can fail"[17].

A psychological factor that lies behind that is described by another French theologian: "Psychology teaches us that time is an essential factor for going beyond the love of self to love of another, for learning to love the other for him or her self"[18].

The consequence of this for Christian marriage has been spelt out by Aubert. Since part of the reality of fidelity, observable both by common experience and psychology, is that it can fail, "therefore if we are going to preserve the doctrine of indissolubility, we need to interpret into it the risk of failure"[19].

An Abandoned Partner

We should now return to the case that set us off on our enquiry, namely someone who has been irrevocably abandoned by the other marriage partner. Forcing him/her to a permanent life of celibacy seemed to conflict with some Scripture and (all?) modern insights into human sexuality. On the other hand it seemed to be demanded by the Church's teaching that all consummated marriages freely entered into are indissoluble.

To try to escape from that impasse, we took the hint from theologians that we should examine the Church's current teaching by looking carefully at three of the human realities it is mainly referring to.

First we saw that if we understand by "marriage" a relationship of love and sharing, then there are unions between Catholics which fitted the traditional Catholic understanding of marriage but do not fit the present one, and in some cases never will. The purpose of Jesus' teaching was to assert that it is profoundly wrong to destroy *marriages*. The possibility that some unions would be incapable of becoming that was not an issue in his time. Today it is. We now seem forced to say either that not all legitimate unions immediately – and in some cases ever – become marriages, or, at the least, that there are very different types and stages of marriage. It is therefore much more difficult to be sure that Jesus' teaching on divorce would, *in every case*, preclude an abandoned partner from entering into another union – whether you prefer to call it "marrying" or "*re*-marrying". May we insist on applying it to such cases, where there is so much responsible doubt, and where a deep and valid human tendency – the need for marriage – is involved?

We then moved to a closely related aspect of the traditional Catholic teaching about marriage: that it consists in exchanging exclusive sexual rights. This is obviously correct. But when we examined what that means in the light of our understanding of sexuality, we were forced to conclude that marriage consists of more than exchanging rights to a merely *physical* act.

Unions where that is all that partners can exchange must be considered either not to be marriages, or, at least, to be lesser kinds of marriages, either permanently or temporarily. This, again, could affect our assessment of the rights of that abandoned partner. If, for instance, he or she has never been involved in what could be called a marriage, it is difficult to see how anybody could legitimately bar that person from marrying now.

We then took up the matter of indissolubility
directly. We reaffirmed the validity of Jesus' insight
that the glory of any marriage is to achieve a complete
and unshakable loving faithfulness. Where that glory is
not achieved, perhaps the greatest glory open to us
departs from the capabilities of our life.

But we had to record strong argument from many
quarters for the view that such loving faithfulness is "a
task, a goal to pursue. And it can fail". And, if it
irrevocably fails, the vital Christian purpose of main-
taining that all consummated Catholic marriages are
indissoluble seems to be of doubtful relevance to *this*
union. Because of either sin or human weakness, it
cannot attain a true fidelity, and therefore cannot show
God's fidelity. *God's* loving faithfulness to us is always
indissoluble. *Ours* – because we are weak and sinful –
can, very obviously, sometimes fail to be so.

This is clearly another factor that may be applicable
to the case of the abandoned partner. It is closely
related to the other two, for love and its strengthening
through sexual intercourse are integral to marriage
faithfulness.

A Couple Still Together

We have also seen that theologians would see implications here for some *married couples who are still
together*. When one or both partners eventually realize
that, in spite of their persistent efforts, a truly marriage
relationship cannot be theirs, on what grounds can the
Church insist that they remain together?

This question would be forced onto us by the very
logic of what we've seen, even if the theologians them-

selves had not raised it. An experienced pastor and theologian describes the kind of situation that we are talking about.

He begins by recalling that married love consists in a number of clearly identifiable components: the couple relating to each other sufficiently at the social, sexual, emotional, intellectual and spiritual levels:

> Each of these needs to be operating at least at a mimimum level if married love is to grow properly and mature. When some of the more important components are absent or ignored or even violated, married love will only be present in a seriously defective form and there is a real danger that it will deteriorate and die. A renewed decision to love will not be enough to stop this happening. The precise factors which are causing the trouble will need to be tackled if there is to be any hope of recovery. However, some of these factors might be outside the control of the couple. For example, despite their willingness to give it another chance, a couple's marriage might still break up simply because they are quite incompatible either sexually or personality-wise. It is possible that a marriage might die, not because the couple were not committed to life-long fidelity, but because they did not know how to love each other[20].

There are other problems about divorcing Catholics that we still have to consider – like whether divorced and re-married Catholics should be barred from the Eucharist. For the moment it will be best to limit ourselves to the two kinds of situations just described.

The question facing us is this. Helped by Scripture and the modern sciences, we now understand marriage, sexuality and marital faithfulness differently. This leads us to question whether Christian teaching, rightly understood, forbids all abandoned partners to (re-) marry and whether it obliges a couple who have been *unable* to save their marriage to remain together.

These are *questions*, not assertions: the whole Church, led by the Pope and bishops, must eventually decide.

But is it legitimate to ask those questions? Do they conflict with Scripture and the Church's central tradition? Since, to a large extent, we have already indirectly reflected on those questions, some brief notes may be sufficient:

1. Christ's purpose was to prevent the desecration of marriages. And by a marriage he understood a union that could grow into a full and intimate sharing.

He gave us not a law, but a fundamental insight into what should be the central reality in most people's lives. But where there is no marriage, how can it be desecrated?

The question being asked is whether there is a marriage to desecrate in the case of an abandoned partner and of a couple who have conscientiously concluded that their union *cannot* grow into anything even approaching a loving and intimate sharing.

2. Paul *did* allow divorce for a Christian whose spouse insisted on separating. The profound value that Jesus' prohibition had pointed to remained most important. But in such a case an adequate context for the Christian to live his or her faith was even more important. "Once

a person has become a Christian she or he acquires the prerogative to live life's most valuable relationships in a Christian way, and therefore to live a Christian marriage"[21].

For many years it has been suggested by Catholics that an interpretation which demands absolutely identical circumstances for every use of this exception is too legalistic and narrow. "The reason for Paul's ruling is not some quality in the deserter (eg., lack of baptism, lack of faith) but something about the Christian, namely, that he is not bound because he has been called to peace." It seems to follow that if a Christian is abandoned by an "un-Christian" spouse, whether baptized or not, the Christian should be declared free[22].

PART 3

What Happens?
What Should Happen?

In a book about divorce, it's as well to remind ourselves that most marriages bring great happiness. That there are difficulties does not surprise us. We'd hardly expect most couples to relate well at all the levels of their personalities without first encountering some problems. These often come from the couple *wanting* to relate deeply: they're just not prepared to settle for being no more than polite fellow-lodgers. And with unselfishness and perseverance, the marriage can be the stronger for the shared struggle with those problems.

Other couples find happiness together beyond their grasp. They had started with great hope; but now their marriage seems to be in ruins. What they valued most has gone, like the death of a loved friend.

Even at that stage, "death" can be changed to life. A skilled counsellor may help them find that there isn't really death at all. It may be quite a "normal" problem, and the couple find it possible, eventually, to cope with it.

Catholics who decide that their marriages can't be saved are faced with several options. They can:

- stay together (perhaps for the sake of the children);
- divorce, and abandon the practice of their faith;
- apply to the Church for the "annulment" of their marriage;
- divorce (and, perhaps, re-marry), but continue to practise their faith so far as the Church allows.

What light does Scripture and the Church's own thinking throw on these last two options? The last twenty years have seen great developments, and there are more to come. We shall recognize, as we follow them, how they are applications – sometimes timid, sometimes bold – of what we have already found in psychology and Scripture.

6.

Applying For an "Annulment"

One must in honesty admit that the theory behind the Church's "annulling" of marriages seems bizarre to many. But *logically*, at least, it is quite straightforward: a consummated marriage cannot be dissolved. Therefore all that the Church can do is to examine whether the marriage ever really existed. If it didn't, it was "null" (i.e. never existed) from the start, so that the partners are free to marry.

To understand this system and the way it is operated, we need to appreciate that we are halfway through a story. Chapter 1 of the story finished near the end of the 1960s; chapter 2 is where we now stand; and the thrusts of Scripture, lived experience, and modern psychology are combining to lead us, in due time, to chapter 3. The pace has been quick; we've gone quite a long way; but there's quite a bit of tension, and even tragedy, about as we wait for the full outcome.

CHAPTER 1

We've often recalled how the Church officially regarded marriage in the 1960s. From the point of view of Church law, marriage was not too dissimilar to my selling you a house. I contract to sell you my house; and you contract to pay me an agreed sum of money. As such it's an impersonal transaction – there's no need for us even to meet. All that's necessary is for each of us to convey to each other the rights that we promised in our contract. When those rights have been transferred, the contract is completed.

In a marriage, as we've seen, the rights promised were primarily sexual intercourse. That was the "commodity" each partner agreed to convey. Once they had done so, the contract was completed and could never be rescinded.

Of course that didn't mean that marriages were lived in that impersonal way! It was simply a low watermark that official teaching had then reached. Through many accidents of fate, it had got quite considerably distanced from the experience of married couples and from Scripture. And modern psychology was still waiting in the wings.

In the meantime this teaching did seem to have the great advantage of shutting the door on divorce. After the first act of sexual intercourse, there was no going back on the "contract". What was fully a marriage, Jesus had forbidden to be dissolved.

CHAPTER 2

Into the story, at this point, enters a revolution. It burst (there is no other word) onto the world stage in Rome, in December 1965, when the Catholic bishops of the world opted, almost unanimously, for a very different understanding of marriage.

Then this revolution spread. What had happened in the minds and hearts of those bishops happened to other individuals throughout the world. All kinds of forgotten Christian truths and values returned to people's consciousness.

The rediscovery was that marriage is a loving union and sharing between two persons. People who get married don't regard marriage as a contract to exchange rights to a *commodity* that they happen to possess: sexual intercourse. They want to give and receive *each other*. Of course that includes sexual rights. But those rights, as the bishop said, are for "expressing and fostering their mutual gift of themselves". They're not something *separate* from their love and their sharing – a mere adjunct to themselves – like a house or a sum of money exchanged by a contract.

Marriage has, indeed, other characteristics. People who marry don't in fact seek out a "*first*" wife or husband: they want their union to be *complete* – to last "till death do us part". And for Christians, this "intimate and loving sharing" (as the bishops called it) is likely to be their main opportunity of being Christ's presence to people – a *sacrament*.

As the bishops went back to their dioceses that December, many of them must have realized that they had started a great wave. True, they had been asked by the Pope not to work out the practical consequences of their pronouncement. The Pope wanted that to be the task of the Church's lawyers. For the first four years, they saw little movement on that front. Some senior lawyers even alleged that nothing much had been really changed. Then the impact of that revolution on the Church's dealing with annulments began to be felt. Since 1969, there has been a gathering momentum. The Church has worked out a very different picture of what constitutes a valid marriage.

As we view this picture taking shape, we notice that it is the work of three artists. There are the Church lawyers, especially in Rome, who develop the law as they judge requests for annulments; then there is the new Code of Church Law, published in 1983; and, lastly, always at the other two contributors' elbows, probing and questioning, are the theologians, professional and lay – the latter being *all* reflecting Christians. Lawyers, law and theologians make up quite a dynamic mixture. But omit any one of them, and this picture goes awry.

What picture of the Church's power to dissolve marriages has this team so far produced?

Since the Church officially teaches that for Catholics there can be no divorce, the only way it can dissolve marriages is to declare that the minimum requirements for a real marriage were not met at the time of the wedding. It made clear in the Vatican Council that more is required than simply the exchange of sexual rights. So the question it has to ask is: What are the *essential* requirements for a real marriage of Catholics, so that if one of the required elements is missing on the wedding day, that marriage is "null"?

What is essentially required is that the partners really wanted and are capable of "an intimate sharing of life and love". That is what the bishops and the new Church law now understand as marriage. If a couple aren't capable of having this kind of interpersonal relationship with each other, this marriage, the Church says, is impossible. And of course we're not talking of just any kind of intimate relationship. It's one that is "for keeps".

What, in more detail, does that involve?

Applying For an "Annulment"

1. *The couple in themselves*

The best place to start is with a couple who are marrying. They are likely to do so because they believe that they will have a fuller kind of life if their *two* selves become largely *one*. From "I" and "You", they want to form a "We". So they open themselves to one another and accept one another, for a complete and permanent partnership.

An immature, dependent person may not have enough self to give for such a full and lasting union. There isn't enough of an "I" to contribute. Each of the partners must have enough self-knowledge and self-identity not to be smothered by childlike dependence on the other, but instead to be able to find his or her fuller self in this life of mutual giving and receiving of two personalities.

Then each partner must maturely consider and then want this marriage. He or she must have been able to form an adequate evaluation of what this life-long sharing with the other partners will involve, and then freely choose that. More developed powers of judgement are obviously required than for choosing a holiday, a house, or even a career. So it's now acknowledged by most Catholic judges that a decision to take up the marriage vocation can only be made by a fairly balanced person. The mind, the feelings, and the ultimate power of choice have to work in good harmony.

As car passengers sometimes find to their cost, its one thing to *want* to be a good driver, and another thing to *be* one. It's no good the couple maturely deciding that this marriage is what they want if one or both is incapable of putting that wish into practice. Here we move from the *intra*-personal requirements to the *inter*-personal, though, inevitably, they shade into one another.

2. *The couple in their relationship*

A Roman judge for annulments described in 1969 how "excessive selfishness shows an 'insufficient self-giving capacity', so that a truly interpersonal relationship becomes very difficult to achieve"[23]. In less demanding relationships than marriage, he pointed out, that person may be popular with many friends and an effective manager in business. But for the full giving and receiving of marriage, that person may be found incapable.

Four years later, another Roman judge looked more broadly at the interrelationship required in a valid marriage: "The most attention must be given", he said, "to that area of a person's inner life in which an interpersonal relationship is undertaken and developed. The focus is particularly on the capacity of establishing an intimate, permanent and exclusive relationship with a particular person until death." And then, with that Christian humanity that is increasingly distinguishing the Church's treatment of people's marriage situations, the judge explains "exclusive". It's not enough that the person is capable of only a forced and burdensome exclusion of other partners: "'exclusive' is to be taken in a positive sense: satisfying to the person, not the kind that becomes a morally intolerable burden"[24].

If we put together what we've seen so far, we notice that four stages of entering into the marriage are all seen as necessary by these Catholic authorities.

First, each partner must have sufficient *command of*

his or her self to be able to share that enrichingly with the different self of the intended partner.

Second, each partner must have adequately *considered* and *evaluated*, not marriage as an idea, or *any* kind of marriage, but an intimate and life-long sharing with this particular person.

Then each partner must *freely choose* to undertake this marriage, not impelled by fear or some kind of neurosis.

And, lastly, he or she must possess the *capacity* to fulfil this undertaking. Roman judges have made it clear that that includes the capacity

- of self-giving
- of giving oneself and accepting this other person just as he or she is
- of sharing in another person's experience
- of being able to collaborate with another person
- of being sensitive to the needs of others
- of being able to maintain an intimate, exclusive and permanent interpersonal relationship – especially at the emotional level[25].

This, then, is what the Church now generally requires for a marriage to have been valid. It bears in mind that the requirements must not be set too high, since marriage is, after all, the vocation of the great majority! But when Church authorities are asked to make a judgement on whether a marriage is null, their attention focuses mainly on these two aspects of the marriage: the couple in themselves, and their interpersonal relationship.

How Can That Be Done?

Having a reasonably clear yardstick is of course not enough. One then has the problem of applying it. Here that largely involves making good judgements about people's personalities and relationships. The kind of guesses that we have to make when we hire someone for a job or decide to trust a salesperson are clearly insufficient when dealing with such matters. The Church tribunals therefore rely very extensively on the assessment of experts in the field of psychology.

In this matter, too, we are seeing developments that have still a long way to go. In the early 1970s, incapacity for the married relationship would only be declared if the person concerned had a psychological illness. By the end of that decade three advances had been made.

First, it was coming to be recognized that "the psychological assumptions which still inspire and dominate our Church law may be as dated as some of the ancient philosophers' physical theories"[26]. Secondly, even some healthy people have a psychological condition that makes a true marriage impossible.

And, thirdly, not just the individual partners but their ability to relate to each other has to be considered.

There is the person, for instance, who can only project onto the other partner childhood feelings for mother or father. This person may well be normal in the rest of his or her life. But because this marriage relationship, at this stage of his or her development, was psychologically impossible, no marriage can have existed. As we'll see in chapter 3, still more fruitful discoveries are yet to come.

Applying For an "Annulment"

"We are certainly in the middle of intense developments in the law. The seeds of change have been planted, but the shape of the tree to come cannot be determined now"[27], wrote one of America's leading Catholic lawyers about the 1983 Code of Laws. That was no wishful thinking. In the most central areas of the new laws about marriage and divorce, major gaps had deliberately been left.

It is worth noticing how central those areas are and how deliberate the gaps left in them for future developments. One law says that "If either or both of the parties by a positive act of the will exclude marriage itself or *any essential element of marriage*, such party contracts invalidly" (Canon 1101.2). "Fine!" we may say. "Here is a clear-cut rule to settle when a marriage is a true one. Just tell us what you mean by 'the essential elements of marriage', and we'll know just where we are."

Instead, we are told no such thing. "Those essential elements are yet to be decided by Church teaching and the reflections of Church judges", wrote the drafters of that law[28].

It's the same with the essential obligations of marriage. Another law declares that those who, for psychological reasons, are unable to assume the essential obligations of marriage are incapable of contracting marriage. We can deduce some of those obligations from other laws, but we're not presented with the full picture. The main one – "the good of the spouses" – is itself left undefined. The reason, quite clearly, is that the full picture is not yet to hand.

But, although we lack the full picture, we do know with some confidence in which directions to pursue it. One is through the light that modern psychology sheds on what the law is groping toward. "Canon law is based on a relatively simple, even simplistic, understanding of the development of the human personality", wrote Professor Örsy[29]. But that is an accident of history, which the Church is seeking to transcend. Psychologists can show us a great deal about the reality of love in marriage, "the good of the spouses", and the essential elements and obligations.

One further thing it shows us – as we saw earlier – is that human relationships can develop, can regress, and even can die. The marriage relationship is not a static thing which you render permanent by making a "contract" of marriage – like giving rights in perpetuity over a piece of land.

Canada's leading church lawyer alluded to this kind of development some years ago. "The teaching of the Church has traditionally been that marriage comes into existence at the moment of consent and that this does not depend on future or contingent events. Yet 'the good of the spouses' might possibly only be demonstrated as the marriage is lived out. Will these two teachings be reconciled in the future?"[30].

This particular church lawyer heads one of the world's finest centres of Church Law – hence, perhaps, that rather muffled conclusion. A more senior canonist was less inhibited. In a speech in 1977 he spoke of how he had become an unwilling "revolutionary" in these matters[31]. Even after the Vatican Council, as a senior professor in Rome, he had taught that the older approaches were the only ones possible. Then eventually he realized that the Council demanded a radically different understanding. As we look at his argument, we are likely to ask ourselves whether he is simply spelling out more boldly what others have merely implied and what we ourselves have already guessed. Does such boldness risk forcing this early growth? Or is it needed if we are to see our way together to help the people concerned?

Professor Huizing began by pointing out something generally agreed. Church law largely looks at marriage and divorce within the framework of a contract. So it lists the contents of what it takes to be promised in a marriage "contract". Each partner promises, in that contract, to assume certain obligations. To judge whether a particular marriage was valid or invalid, it asks two questions: Did both partners freely choose, on their wedding day, to assume those obligations? And were they both capable of fulfilling them? If the answers are "yes", then the marriage satisfies these yardsticks of the law: it is therefore "valid", and can never be dissolved. The fact that in most of the cases these judges will be asked to hear the marriage broke up long before and there has been a second marriage (with obligations to spouse and perhaps children) can make no difference to their decision. What satisfied a yardstick, satisfies it! There is no more to say.

But, this lawyer asks, *can* a legal yardstick be an adequate one for marriages? In an interpersonal relationship, of course there are rights. He reminded his audience, at the Conference where he gave this speech, that rights existed between him and them in *their* relationship. They had the right to his respect, his kindly intentions to them, his honesty in what he said to them.

As Christians, they had the right to his accepting them as his sisters and brothers in Christ.

But could those rights be secured *by contract*? Could anyone compel them to be fulfilled by any law? If the professor had contracted, before the Conference, to treat his audience in that way, but had then decided not to do so, the Conference organizers could have decided to withold his fee. But they couldn't possibly say plausibly: "That respectful interrelationship exists, that is certainly the case because Professor Huizing promised it, and he is psychologically capable of such a relationship"! All they could say – truly and profoundly – is that the professor has been false to himself, you and us.

In a marriage, the partners promise to be "true till death do us part". By entering marriage – and, particularly, Christian marriage – they are giving each other, any children, the Church, and the world, a solemn promise to do everything they can to achieve indissolubility. That fact is in no way doubted. What is being questioned is whether indissolubility is simply "there" because of that promise.

"Marriage understood as a personal relationship", Huizing wrote, "is not something that can be defined and settled by law. It is a human reality, subject to human change, whether to good or bad, to the more perfect or the less perfect, towards real and lived indissolubility or towards failure. If marriage is regarded as a contract, indissolubility is something that automatically arises from marriage itself or from what you are legally obliged to promise to give in it. But if marriage is regarded primarily as an interpersonal relationship, indissolubility is a 'law' which directs the evolution of the human union of the couple"[32].

And what happens if there *is* failure? Church law and teaching says that the marriage still stands. So do some fine theologians who would say that each partner, even if irrevocably separated for years, still owe marriage faithfulness to each other.

Is that the view the Church should continue to take? Or is it enough to stress that the original marriage promise will always remain a key reality in both partners' lives, but not one that binds them to their marriage?

Huizing is sure that the latter view would be right. "It must be admitted," he said, "that according to Church law there can really exist a marriage which is no more than the incapacity of two people to conclude a marriage, based on their marriage agreement given in one occasion, while their only relationship is to maintain for the rest of their life the incapacity for the other"[33].

If the Church were eventually to share that view, would it lead to chaos and even more distress than at present? If the law cannot measure whether or not a marriage still exists, will that lead to individuals and couples being encouraged to decide that for themselves, often at difficult times in their relationship, when their judgement is clouded by rows or other problems?

Here we obviously have a very serious issue. It is part of the wider question about the way in which Catholic divorce should be handled. Huizing has some proposals to make about that, as have several others. Their views can be surveyed in the next chapter.

7.

Who Should Decide About Divorce?

Who decides at present?

In 1977, in the U.S.A., there were six million divorced Catholics. That same year, fewer than nineteen thousand divorce cases were dealt with by the Church authorities. So the vast majority of cases simply divorce and remarry, without application to the Church, and in conflict with its teaching.

Before coming back to that fact and trying to assess its significance, we should first complete our picture. What about those nineteen thousand cases? How are their applications dealt with? And is the present system the right one?

First, the present system is a *legal* one. Its job is the impartial application of the law of the Church, and it is operated by officials such as judges and advocates, few of whom are married, and hardly any of whom are women. What these people are dealing with is marriages where, usually, much suffering has been experienced. Since their business is to apply law – not to offer a service like counselling – there has to be a formal kind of procedure, with both sides of the case argued out and with the questioning of the witnesses. After sifting all the evidence it can acquire, the tribunal eventually decides whether this marriage seems to have satisfied the Church's requirements for a valid marriage at the time of the wedding – it has no power, of course, to declare that although it does seem to have satisfied those requirements, it has now clearly "died". In the U.S.A. the decision is usually reached in about a year, and in almost all cases that decision is that the marriage *appears* to have been invalid* (*certainty* is never claimed). In countries like the United Kingdom a smaller majority of decisions reach that conclusion, and the process is apt to take about two years.

In this century – and particularly since the 1970s – there have been enormous developments in the way these tribunals operate. Until the 1920s, the existence of these tribunals was unknown to almost all lay Catholics. Compulsive readers of Catholic Directories would, it is true, find that their diocese had one, and a galaxy of senior clerics would be listed as composing it. But few if any marriages were even proposed to it for judgement.

Even in the 1960s, the situation had not much changed. In the diocese of Brooklyn, for example, the first ever affirmative decision had been given in 1943, and in 1968 the number was still only fourteen – even in that large New York area! Already, however, the seeds of great change had begun to be planted. In 1949, the Brooklyn tribunal heard its first case that turned on psychological evidence.

It was not until 1970 that the diocese began to consider what it calls "greater numbers". Then gradually, over that decade, occurred the change we've already seen. As in Rome itself, and in other dioceses, it began to be recognized by the Brooklyn marriage judges, that

---

* A much smaller proportion of such decisions in the U.S.A. is anticipated in future years.

one did not have to be psychologically ill to have a personality disorder that made one incapable of marriage.

Even well into the 1970s, the effect of this discovery was muted. A Brooklyn judge described why in 1978:

> For many years psychiatrists had been telling us that these personality disorders frequently are more disruptive of the common conjugal life than psychoses or neuroses. At that time, this meant very little to us because we did not look upon the ability to lead a common conjugal life as an element of the marriage contract[34].

As the 1970s advanced, the Roman decisions would give increasing cause for taking that to be an essential element – ultimately to be confirmed by the new 1983 laws.

As it increasingly worked with psychologists over the 1970s, a tribunal would greatly increase its awareness of the relevance of that science. It wasn't a question of a greater sympathy for someone with such a disorder or of becoming more permissive. Two factors help to make that clear. First, psychology was showing the tribunals that a person with such disorders "only has an evaluative knowledge of his/her own rights and no real concept of his/her obligations towards another, or the rights of another". It wasn't just a matter of unfortunate patterns of behaviour, which a Christian spouse should be expected to regard with love and sympathy, but of what can be called, in compressed language, a "lack of internal integrity which makes an internal interpersonal integrity impossible"[35].

And the second thing Brooklyn found was that when those applying for nullity went for psychological testing at the suggestion of tribunal officials, they "revealed very, very frequently the presence of severe pathology"[36].

This, then, is the system we have and the way it now generally operates. The question that arises is whether a system devised to cope with a different kind of Church, is the best for our own times.

Ten years ago an American Professor of Church Law was already raising two major questions about this:

1. "Can a pre-eminently clerical nullity process realistically meet the pastoral needs of married couples or elicit their whole-hearted co-operation?"

2. "The present process is too strongly based on a conflict of rights situation. . . . Generally the petitions in marriage cases in most English-speaking countries are primarily . . . concerned about peace of conscience and full participation in the sacramental life of the Church . . . A sincere desire to rebuild their lives in Christ prompts most petitioners to approach the court. So the decision about marital validity must be a primarily religious one situated within the broader context of ministry to the divorced"[37].

In response to the professor's first question, probably most of us – including members of the Church tribunals – would welcome much greater lay involvement in them. The job specification, in terms of intelligence, training, and sensitivity to people's character and feelings, is rightly very high. At present far too small a number of often very gifted and kindly people cope as well as they can within the system prescribed.

The proposals made in the second point go deeper than simply more lay involvement and raise the whole question of what "Church" should in practice mean to us in situations of marriage difficulty and even failure.

We are living at a time when, in perhaps most local Christian communities, our theology has enormously outrun our practice. Until well into the 1960s, almost all of us had an understanding of the Church where, for instance, a parish priest was expected to be an absolute monarch. Now almost all of us have outgrown that. We have graduated to the much more authentic theology of the New Testament, which is centred on fellowship and community. But given the size and the other circumstances of most parishes, there is often very little community in them. There isn't the high degree of mutual encouragement, support, and correction in our spiritual journey that were the central fibre of Christian life as the New Testament envisaged it.

A Catholic couple with marriage difficulties may live in a parish with a counselling service. Such services are often known to help couples heal apparently "hopeless" situations. In that case "Church", when they need it most, isn't primarily a group of judges and advocates who apply a long legal process, however kindly, in the diocesan chancery. To some extent at least, "Church" is your sisters and brothers who lend a hand when you need them. And "theology" is no longer notional and idealistic descriptions: it helps you make sense of and appreciate the good things you have.

Until that kind of situation is present in a locality, will an adequately Christian way of dealing with marital breakdown and divorce be really possible?

Where such a situation is present, however, great possibilities arise. In that context, the suggestion made by Professor Huizing and others would seem a most desirable procedure:

The Church's chief concern would no longer be juridical questions, like validity and invalidity, or indissolubility and dissolubility, but pastoral concern for the people involved in their personal situations. Every effort would be made to ensure that Christians would be helped to better understand and appreciate the significance and the human and Christian values of marriage.

It would be stressed that concern for fidelity in marriage and the stability of families is a matter for the whole Church community; the members of the community are called to help each other, when the need arises.

When a marriage seems to have definitively failed, the spouses, if they wish to continue to take part in the life and worship of the Church, haven't the right to impose their unilateral decision on the Christian community. . . . The judgement of the Church would not be a juridical judgement, but one that is human and spiritual, fitted to the real possibilities of the people in question.

There would be in each diocese one or more teams whose members would include people well versed in pastoral psychology, etc. They would work very personally and confidentially, at the level of conscience. One member of the team would have the responsibility to speak with the couple, separately, and, if possible, together.

They would be absolutely clear that the purpose is, above all, to help the spouses themselves to reach decisions that are humanly and spiritually acceptable, not to impose already-made decisions. This member would then discuss the situation with at least two other members of the team.

It would be possible to appeal from their decision, even twice if required. An appeal to the Holy See would be possible.

The judgements of the teams would range, according to the case, from a decision that any kind of separation would be unacceptable, to one that allowed another marriage, or one that tolerated a second (civil) marriage without barring the persons involved from the sacraments[38].

8.

Must the Marriage Be In Church?

We can now turn to Catholics in two other typical
situations connected with divorce:

1. John and Elizabeth were baptized Catholics in in-
fancy. Until adolescence they attended church on
Sunday, but without enthusiasm. They would tell you,
in all sincerity, that Christian faith, at present, meant
very little to them. They learnt very little about it either
at home or at school; and, so far, it had not "spoken" to
their lives.

A few years ago, they decided to get married. Both
sets of parents are "regular", though unenthusiastic,
Catholics. Elizabeth and John, mainly for social
reasons, still count themselves as Catholics. As a result,
they got married in a Catholic church.

Simply because they had both been baptized and
were married in a Catholic church, this is officially
regarded as a sacrament.

Until recently, the assertion that John and
Elizabeth's marriage is a sacrament would have struck
hardly anyone as strange. They had been baptized; and
they "took part in a sacrament". What's the problem?

But the Church, as we have seen, no longer understands
a sacrament primarily as a rite you take part in. The
sacrament of marriage is putting into effect a decision to
try to embody the life and loving faithfulness of God.

In the rite itself, you will publicly express and celebrate that decision. Of course that's important. But the most important part of the sacrament is your *living* that decision. A church lawyer expressed the point succinctly many years ago: "The sacraments are not so much the act of getting married or baptized or ordained, but the living state of being married, being baptized and being ordained, etc."[39].

We've seen that in that church ceremony, John and Elizabeth had no intention of making any such decision. With so little faith, how could they?

The conclusion from this seems obvious: their marriage cannot be a sacrament. No one should ask them to pretend that it is. Obviously they have as much right to get married as anyone else. But, while they have insufficient faith to believe that Christian marriage is a sacrament, their marriage should be a civil one. Later, perhaps, faith will take root and grow. Then they can be welcomed into embracing Christian marriage.

Misgivings

Although it seems impossible to fault the theological logic of that conclusion, misgivings naturally arise.

It seems to recommend such a break in our tradition of Christians always marrying in church. But when we dig a bit into history, we find that to be not so old a custom.

Until 11th November 1563, Catholics did not have to marry in church or even before a priest. At that point, the Council of Trent decided that they must. But its motive was merely practical: it wanted marriages recorded, because otherwise disputes arose. The obvious person to do that was the priest – often the only literate person in a parish. Today, the motive for Trent's decision is no longer valid, now that the state records marriages. So tradition isn't really an obstacle.

Then there is a deeper misgiving. Wouldn't encouraging some Catholics to marry civilly make an easy gateway to divorce? Not really. Jesus, we have seen, was not talking about Christian marriages when he said they should be permanent. Anyone who dismisses his or her spouse is being radically untrue to him or her self, and to the spouse, and to marriage as a human reality. A civil marriage, in other words, is just as indissoluble as a Church one.

But there's an even more important reply to that misgiving. Suppose that there *are* disadvantages to letting Catholics with insufficient faith marry civilly. Would that justify asking them to promise solemnly before the Church to do something with their whole future lives that is beyond their power? Christian marriage is a covenant, a solemn and loving agreement, between God and a Christian couple. "To assume that a covenant between God and the couple could come into existence even if the couple had no faith in God's action is as absurd as to think that a covenant could have arisen between God and Abraham even if Abraham refused to believe"[40]. Can we ask John and Elizabeth publicly to proclaim and celebrate a non-existent covenant?

The chief thing to be said for the proposal, therefore, is that to allow Christians of inadequate faith to marry only civilly seems the only honest course possible in a matter of great importance. And there are additional advantages.

One is that it would help make clearer the real purpose of Christian marriage. It expresses a couple's faith – or the faith of one of them, St Paul would say, if it is allowed gently and humanly to transform the other (1 Corinthians 7:12–14). It expresses their whole stance to God and to the years of their life together. They express this before the Christian community. This Christian marriage and family life will enrich that community. And the couple have the right to the community's support, particularly in difficult times.

It is not only couples with faith, but also those at present without it who could gain from this. It invites the seeds of faith in them to grow as adult and free. They will often have come from homes and schools where Christian life is, at best, shallow. As they get older, and as children and other responsibilities come, an adult faith may become more possible. Then, freely, they can adopt Christian marriage – not as a decoration for a wedding ceremony, but for what it really is.

An important aspect of this proposal is that, although it is widely seen as theologically unassailable, it contradicts one of the 1983 laws: "A valid marriage contract cannot exist between baptized persons without its being by that very fact a sacrament" (1055.2).

This is simply a repetition of the 1917 law, and was left in the new Code of Law because the drafters did not feel it was their job to settle theological questions. What this highlights is that in fundamental matters of theology, we are to some extent today in a kind of twilight zone. The bishops of the Vatican Council were told not to tackle theological questions about marriage, and the drafters of the 1983 Laws felt them to be outside their brief. Yet *how* we answer such questions, and *whether* we address them, profoundly affects our Christian living.

One result is that many Catholics have not had a chance to understand and evaluate this proposal. Until they can, any implementation will have to be particularly careful not to shock them.

2. Peter and Jane are Catholics and decide to get married. Both of them are under twenty-one, and they are aware from the divorce statistics and from the marriages of some of their contemporaries that the permanent commitment they sincerely intend may not in fact last. A friend advised them to get married in a registry office: "If it works well, you can get it put right by the Church later. But if it doesn't work out, and you divorce, you'll be able to marry Catholics if you wish, because the Church regards a marriage of Catholics in a registry office as invalid."

If Peter and Jane take that advice, they will be adopting a method that is often used by Catholics who want a trial marriage. If the marriage doesn't succeed, one or both may wish to marry another Catholic. Because the Church regards civil marriage by Catholics as invalid, it holds that they are free to do so. So, Catholics and non-Catholics find a Church resolutely forbidding divorce to some, but happily remarrying these married people!

If the proposal to accept the validity of civil marriages were accepted, this situation could not arise. Peter and Jane would know that, from the Church's point of view, their choice of a civil or a Church marriage would not affect the validity. If they eventually decided on divorce, and wanted the Church to sanction a second marriage, their marriage, in whichever form, would need to be considered and judged by those empowered to do so.

9.

The Divorced-Remarried
and the Eucharist

The present law is well known. A Catholic whose first marriage was valid and who remarried after a divorce, is not allowed to receive communion. For many Catholics this is indeed a sorrow and impoverishment.

I think of my friend Dick. He got married at nineteen, when he was immature and rather selfish. He and Alice had six children and remained married for twenty years, but they were clearly very incompatible. Even Dick's parents – very "conservative" Catholics – told me that they were glad that the couple eventually divorced.

Dick has been matured by his years of unhappiness. He and Elizabeth, his second wife, are happily married; they are good parents to the children from both the marriages; and Dick now wishes to live as a good Catholic for his own sake, for Elizabeth's (not yet a Catholic) and his children's. Elizabeth quite often accompanies Dick to Sunday Mass. But Dick cannot take communion except in a rather distant parish, by private arrangement with the priest.

In our first chapter we heard Archbishop Worlock of Liverpool asking his fellow bishops in the 1980 Rome Synod, in the name of the bishops of England and Wales, about cases like Dick's: "Many pastors nowadays are faced with Catholics whose first marriages have perished and who have now a second and more stable . . . union. . . . Often such persons, especially in their desire to help their children, long for the restoration of full eucharistic communion with the Church and its Lord. Is this spirit of repentance and desire for sacramental strength to be forever frustrated?" The Pope, at the end of the Synod, reiterated the former law. Inspite of that, "the papal statement headed into rather heavy weather – a virtually unanimous theological opinion that some divorced and remarried people may be admitted to the sacraments"[41].

Of course this isn't the first time that a Pope has believed one thing and that most theologians have believed something different. *Humanae Vitae* is the most obvious example. Another is the present Pope's encyclical on the ordination of women. Provided we still give full weight to the Pope's leadership, it is even healthy, since it helps to remind us that the Church is a body, not a dictatorship. It is also likely to suggest to us that there are important issues at stake and that a "solution" may not be quick or easy.

Before we consider the directions in which Catholics are seeking a solution to this problem, it is worth noting the distance the Church has already travelled in this matter.

In the last century, Pius IX said that the divorced-remarried were in a state of concubinage. There was nothing that resembled Christian marriage in their relationship. Yet today the Church urges them to attend Mass and to deepen their prayer life. "They should be encouraged to play as full a part as possible in the life of the local parish", said the bishops of England and

Wales[42]. "They should be made to feel welcome within the Church community", said the Bishop of Richmond[43]. God's grace is therefore recognized to be in them.

If a solution to our problem is to be found, it may depend on our being clear as to *why* these people, whom we are now officially encouraged to welcome into the community and regard as endowed with God's grace, are not allowed to receive the Eucharist. It is *not* a judgement on their having divorced and remarried. If a person is responsible for endangering or breaking up a marriage, of course that is a very serious sin. But repentance restores us to God's friendship. And we are obviously talking here only of those who have repented.

The only reason that can plausibly be proposed today for the prohibition is that Catholics would deduce from the fact of the Church rescinding it, that the Church now approves of divorce and remarriage.

We have already noticed grounds for taking this argument very seriously. The Church, we saw, is "almost the only relevant reality in society today that has the moral authority to represent this fundamentally Christian faithfulness in marriage"[44]. This ability, moreover, is gravely under threat. In 1963, forty-one per cent of American Catholics in their twenties believed divorce to be wrong; in 1974, only seventeen per cent of that age group; and in 1979 only eleven per cent of them. It is therefore asserted that "changing our discipline regarding readmission to Penance and the Eucharist . . . may at this time be seen as the Church reversing its teaching and now blessing divorce and remarriage"[45].

Everyone, I think, agrees that if (or while) it is the case that changing the present discipline *would* be interpreted in that way, this change would be wrong. But could it be made clear that such a change signifies no such thing? Is it even urgent that we do so? There are reasons to believe that we must urgently face these questions.

We can start that by seeing what change is being proposed. No one is proposing that the admission of the divorced-remarried to the sacraments should be easy or automatic. Each case would have to be judged on its merits with the help of such questions as these:

1. In this second marriage, is the couple fulfilling the responsibilities of the first and second unions?
2. How committed is their Christian life?
3. Are they not simply avoiding scandal, but positively contributing to building up Christian married life in the community?[46]

So what the theologians want to see achieved is that Catholics in general should be enabled to see that admitting Catholics *such as these* to the sacraments is desirable, and that that does not sanction divorce. "We must maintain the radical nature of the permanence of marriage, but also the radical character of mercy in the faith community"[47].

There are several ways in which we could work to change perceptions in this matter; though to succeed they would probably need to march together.

1. **Helping Catholics appreciate the psychological realities of marriage**. This could greatly help them in

deepening their own marriage relationships and in overcoming their marital problems. It would also help them to appreciate what may have led to the divorce and remarriage of some of the couples in question.

2. **Helping Catholics better appreciate the message of Scripture on this matter**. At present it comes across to many Catholics as an absolute law intended for Christians only, not as a profoundly true insight into marriage which every married Catholic has a grave responsibility to live up to (but in some cases will not be able to).

3. **Helping Catholics understand why points 1. and 2. are leading to considerable developments in theology and official practice**. The expression of conflicting opinions within the Church on marriage and divorce is causing disquiet[48]. Catholics need to enter into the discussion; but so far most lack the tools to do so. They therefore cannot, for example, appreciate that a purely "contract" view of marriage is: (a) receding, for good reasons; (b) to the extent that it lasts, preventing the Church confronting the fact that marriages can fail.

4. **Increasing the role of the local community**. Most of us learn through activity much more than we do through instruction. Also, Catholic couples are called to live out Christ's teaching, not just as individual couples, but as part of his "body": the local Christian community.

For both these reasons, progress largely depends on the local community mutually supporting each other's marriages. Those it particularly charges with this responsibility could help the community to reflect on the developing Christian insights that psychology and Scripture have made possible, so that they can the better appraise the situations of specific couples.

One of the most important insights, for our present purposes, is that a sacrament is *not* – as is widely assumed – *only* to express unity in belief, but also a means of healing and grace. The local community's concern for its divorced-remarried members will make them more aware of those who *want* healing and grace, and that will "give flesh" to that insight.

This will greatly enrich our own reception of the sacraments. We won't do so as "virtuous" people who are *full* members of the Church, while the divorced-remarried are barely members at all, or "outsiders". "We are a pilgrim Church, in need of sacramental sustenance . . . precisely because we are weak, are sinners, are only more or less possessed by the faith we profess"[49]. We are alongside these people, not "above", in a different class. In spite of parables like *The Pharisee and the Publican*, perhaps all of us are sometimes prone to take the stance Jesus condemned there. We forget that it was so often the sinners who recognized their need for God's kindness and were therefore able to receive Jesus.

The implications of this were spelt out for us in 1981 by Bernard Häring, the doyen of Catholic moral theologians:

The whole Church and especially its pastoral leaders must be for the divorced a sacrament of God's healing and merciful love. Concrete rules such as excluding the divorced from the sacraments are subordinate to this basic concern, because concrete rules are precisely vehicles for this basic concern. A sudden change in this practical norm without previous change to a more healing attitude would only make things worse[50].

But Dick and his family, and millions like them, still have to wait. Already in England in 1980, almost every report from the dioceses "makes an urgent plea for a re-examination of present policy in this matter"[51]. But is that really possible? Is it not probable that in another twenty years such urgent pleas will be widely heard, but fruitlessly?

The parish priest, officially, is powerless in this matter – and clandestine action cannot change the general situation. The bishop is powerless – he cannot step out of line. And Rome is also powerless: you can't beat Pharisaism with encyclicals or synods.

Only the local diocese and parish – in a less centralized Church – can judge when specific communities have done enough to transform themselves into sacraments of God's healing love.

And what a target to set them! The Pharisaism in all of us is partly our human weakness and partly our inheritance from an era of legalism. Most of us are aware of people like Dick, and would like to help them. How good for us to know that we're not yet ready to do that! We have, as a parish, to hear the Gospel message again so as to shed a little of our righteousness and become genuine Christians: people like Christ, for Dick, for his family, and for so many others.

Notes

1. Especially in his *Marriage, Faith and Love*, London, 1981.
2. *ibid.*, p. 40.
3. *ibid.*, p. 76.
4. e.g. Joseph Fitzmyer (1976): "(not intended) to be understood absolutely"; Joachim Gnilka (1979); Walter Kasper (1980); John L. McKenzie (1980); Jerome Murphy-O'Connor (1981): Paul considered it not as a binding precept but as a significant directive; Peter Stuhlmacher (1982); Helmut Merklein (1983): Paul did not understand it as a Law; P. Rémy (1983): "not a juridical law, but an ethical one"; Theodore Mackin (1984); Joseph Zmizewski (1984).
5. Gerhard Friedrich, *Sexualität und Ehe*, Stuttgart, 1977, p. 147.
6. Gerhard Lohfink, *Jesus and Community*, London, 1984, p. 62.
7. Walter Kasper, *Theology of Christian Marriage*, London, 1980, p. 64.
8. George MacRae, "New Testament Perspectives on Marriage and Divorce", in James J. Young (ed.), *Ministering to the Divorced Catholic*, New York, 1979, pp. 38, 47.
9. Gregory Baum, "The Magisterium in a Changing Church", *Concilium* 1967, pp. 39-40 (slightly amended).
10. Valentine Peter, "Divorce, Remarriage and the Sacraments", *Jurist* 1982, p. 125.
11. Walter Kasper, *op. cit.*, p. 64.
12. *ibid.*, p. 2.
13. George MacRae, *art. cit.*, p. 47.
14. Walter Kasper, *op. cit.*, p. 26.
15. *op. cit.*, p. 96.

16. *ibid.*, p. 95.
17. Jean-Marie Aubert, "Pratique Canonique et Sens de l'humain", *Revue de droit canonique* 1978, p. 103 (condensed).
18. Albert Desserprit, "Durée-Fidelité", *Vie-Spirituelle – Supplement* 1980, p. 514.
19. Jean-Marie Aubert, *art. cit.*, pp. 103–4.
20. Kevin T. Kelly, *Divorce and Remarriage*, London, 1982, pp. 32–3.
21. Theodore Mackin, *Divorce and Remarriage*, New York, 1984, p. 10.
22. Brian Byron, "General Theology of Marriage in the New Testament etc.", *Australasian Catholic Record* 1972, pp. 2–9.
23. Quoted in: James B. Zusy, "Matrimonial Consent and Immaturity", *Studia Canonica* 1981, p. 215.
24. *ibid.*, pp. 218–20 (Serrano's judgements, partly paraphrased).
25. *ibid.*, pp. 234–5.
26. Ladislas Örsy, "Matrimonial Consent in the New Code", *Jurist* 1983, p. 52.
27. *ibid.*, p. 62.
28. Quoted in A. Mendonça, "The Nature of Matrimonial Consent", *Studia Canonica* 1982, p. 82, n. 21.
29. *art. cit.*, p. 43.
30. Frank Morissey, "Revising Church Legislation on Marriage", *Origins* 1979, p. 212.
31. Peter Huizing, "La conception du mariage dans le Code, etc.", *Revue de droit canonique* 1977, pp. 135–46.
32. *ibid.*, p. 142.
33. *ibid.*, p. 143.
34. Marion Reinhardt, "The Emphasis in American Tribunals", *Ephemerides Iuris Canonici* 1978, p. 69.
35. *ibid.*, p. 70.
36. *ibid.*, p. 68.
37. Thomas Green, "A Living Jurisprudence", *Concilium* 1977, n. 107, pp. 50–1.
38. *art. cit.*, pp. 144–6 (abbreviated, and slightly paraphrased).

39. Michael Ashdowne, "A Study of the Sacramentality of Marriage", *Studia Canonica* 1975, p. 299.
40. Ladislas Örsy, "Faith, Sacrament, Covenant and Christian Marriage, etc.", *Theological Studies* 1982, p. 386.
41. Richard McCormick, "Notes on Moral Theology", *Theological Studies* 1982, pp. 119–20.
42. In their *Easter People* 1980, n. 110.
43. Quoted in Richard McCormick, "Notes on Moral Theology", *Theological Studies* 1981, p. 123.
44. Walter Kasper, *op. cit.*, p. 64.
45. Valentine Peter, *art. cit.*, p. 134.
46. James Provost, "Reconciliation of Catholics in Second Marriages", *Origins* 1978, pp. 204–8.
47. Richard McCormick, *art. cit.*, in *Theological Studies* 1982, p. 120.
48. *Synod 87: Summary of the Consultation*, English and Welsh Bishops' General Secretariat, London, 1986, p. 14.
49. Richard McCormick, "Indissolubility and the Right to the Eucharist", in James Young (ed.) *op. cit.*, p. 77.
50. Bernard Häring, writing in *Theologie der Gegenwart* 1981, as paraphrased by Richard McCormick, *art. cit.* in *Theological Studies* 1982, p. 122.
51. Diocesan Reports for the English and Welsh National Pastoral Congress 1980: *Liverpool*, Slough, 1981, p. 68.